Peter Lund Simmonds

The Commercial Letter Writer

A Series of Modern and Practical Letters of Business, Trade Circulars and Forms

Peter Lund Simmonds

The Commercial Letter Writer
A Series of Modern and Practical Letters of Business, Trade Circulars and Forms

ISBN/EAN: 9783744726696

Printed in Europe, USA, Canada, Australia, Japan

Cover: Foto ©Suzi / pixelio.de

More available books at **www.hansebooks.com**

THE

COMMERCIAL

LETTER WRITER:

A SERIES OF

MODERN AND PRACTICAL LETTERS OF BUSINESS,

TRADE CIRCULARS, FORMS, &c.

SELECTED FROM ACTUAL MERCANTILE CORRESPONDENCE.

BY

P. L. SIMMONDS,

AUTHOR OF A "DICTIONARY OF TRADE PRODUCTS," "THE COMMERCIAL
PRODUCTS OF THE VEGETABLE KINGDOM," AND NUMEROUS
OTHER WORKS ON TRADE AND COMMERCE.

LONDON:
GEORGE ROUTLEDGE AND SONS,
BROADWAY, LUDGATE HILL;
NEW YORK: 416, BROOME STREET.

PREFACE.

THE vast extension of British Commerce, the increased facilities of telegraphic communication, and the rapidity of action thus necessitated, have materially altered the character of business correspondence, especially in London and the large manufacturing towns and shipping ports.

Commercial letters now are usually of the briefest character, except with some few Foreign Houses on regular Foreign Mail days. Indeed, orders and communications are mostly carried on by memoranda of a few lines, written on slips with printed headings. Stiff, formal business letters are, therefore, quite out of fashion, and those used very different to the pedantic and precise letters which are usually put forth as guides to business correspondence.

As affording fairer samples of commercial letters— although they may not reach the ambitious style of pedantic authorities—I have preferred selecting various *bonâ fide* letters from a large mass of correspondence, to concocting special models. Although these may not be adapted to all wants, yet they will at least serve as guides in a variety of cases, for a great deal must necessarily be left to

the tact and judgment of the writer, who, in this educated
age, will usually be able, in a very short time, to promptly
meet any emergency.

I have reprinted a few useful forms, because in some
places these may not always be obtainable.   It has been
usual in works of this class to append a list of commercial
abbreviations, technicalities, and definitions of mercantile
phrases, but I have thought this quite unnecessary, because
these are all given in my "Dictionary of Trade Products,
Commercial, Manufacturing, and Technical Terms, &c.,"
a cheap standard work, issued by the same publishers,
and which has long been in use in the office or counting-
house of nearly every merchant, broker, and shipping
agent.

P. L. SIMMONDS.

CONTENTS.

II.—LETTERS TO FOREIGN CORRESPONDENTS.

III.—APPLICATIONS FOR MONEY, REPLIES, &c.

IV.—LETTERS RESPECTING SHIPMENTS, &c.

V.—BUSINESS LETTERS ON INTERNATIONAL EXHI-
BITION MATTERS.

VI.—TRADE CIRCULARS AND NOTICES, &c.

VII.—BUSINESS FORMS, &c.

COMMERCIAL LETTER-WRITER.

——◦◦◦——

(Letter on Cotton Cultivation in Brazil.)

TEMPLE LODGE, HAMMERSMITH,
26th June, 1862.

MY DEAR SIR,—I regret exceedingly I could not have the pleasure of seeing you before you left town. Engagements held me bound, all Friday and Saturday, so that I was absolutely prevented from keeping my appointment, which I much regret, as I was very anxious to ascertain your views on the practical means of increasing the growth of Brazilian cotton. I have no idea of the extent of land now employed in the northern provinces in this cultivation, beyond the rough guess founded on the official returns of the quantities exported up to 1858, which, on the average of the last three years, appear to have been annually rather more than $33\frac{3}{4}$ million pounds. Now, in India we learn that some soils produce 150 lb., others 300 lb. per acre. Let us presume that in Brazil the yield is 100 lb. per acre, the number of acres cultivated would thus be 166,400. That the country is

B

capable of extending the cultivation over an immense space favourable to this branch of industry, and of producing a very considerably increased amount of cotton, there can be no doubt; but the limit to this exists in the difficulty of finding a sufficient number of hands, where the labourers are nearly all slaves. Projects have been formed for bringing coolies from India, or Chinese, in which plans the Brazil Government has shown great willingness to afford succour, in some instances; but the jealousies of our Anti-Slavery Societies placed a bar against their adoption. The report that will now go out of the market value of the very poor samples of Brazilian cotton sent to the International Exhibition, and the certainty of the cessation of further supplies from America, will no doubt stimulate many Haciendeiros in the northern provinces to extend the cultivation of this staple; and we may be sure that not only the central, but each provincial government will do all in their power to facilitate this industry. This matter is now, however, resolving itself into a world wide competition, and must be attended with some risk to the Brazilian when we see the numerous samples of cotton now brought together from all tropical parts of the globe. In regard to your inquiry about the cost of cotton, we find the average price it fetched in the port of Brazil during 1856-7-8 was 6 dls. 040 per arroba; and as the exchange during that time ruled above the par of 27d., we may safely take the value in sterling, delivered in those ports, at about 5d. per lb. during three years.

I had hoped for the favour of obtaining from you some information respecting the kinds of cotton you would recommend for cultivation in Brazil, or those likely to prove most remunerative to the growers, and also any hints as to the manner of preparing it for the market. I have long had my eye on the Macarthy gin, with its improvements. I believe it is not unknown in the Province of Pernambuco, but I suspect the old saw-gin still prevails in the interior, though it will no doubt gradually disappear when the value of the other becomes more known.

You mention the two bales from Hayti as being the kinds most needed. I cannot now call to mind their quality, out of the great number of samples exhibited, but I will again look at them attentively. I fancy they were both long staple,—one of high price. I imagine, however, that your greatest demand will always be for good short staple. Your advice on these points will be of much value. When you say you require two millions of bales of each of the two qualities, I presume you mean this as the Manchester annual demand from all parts of the world, and that you estimate a bale at 300 lb. weight. You must of course know well the qualities of the kinds known in the market as Bahias, Pernams, Maceios, Maranhams, &c. Would you recommend any change in the sort of seed to be cultivated in those provinces, or do you consider them to be sufficiently good of their kind? When I had last the pleasure of seeing you, I think you said your Association would willingly supply cotton-seed of different kinds. Will you have the goodness to state if this be so, and at what price for various qualities? The Brazilian Government seems to think that by the use of improved implements the cultivation may be greatly ameliorated. I am inclined to think that much good might result from the introduction of better implements, provided the local administration could be induced to teach them their use and application, otherwise, in the hands of ignorant blacks, their introduction would, I think, be useless.

I am, my dear Sir,

Very truly yours,

W. WANKLYN, Esq.   JOHN MIERS.

(Reply Reporting on Qualities of Cotton, &c.)

BURY, LANCASHIRE, 16th July, 1862.

MY DEAR SIR,—I trust that you will not have thought I had forgotten my promise, but I really up to this time have been so busy with my Report that I have not had leisure to answer yours of the 26th ult. with the consideration it deserves and requires. In a few days you shall have a copy (more if required) of the Report, and by it you will see that there is no fear of Brazil dreading an over production of cotton from other sources, for the total supply from all sources, including India and excluding the United States, does not, or rather cannot, this year exceed 1,500,000 bales, and we require above 4,000,000 to supply the united requirements of this country and the Continent. The great obstacle to a successful—i. e. paying crop, will, I am sure, be only a temporary one. It consists simply of the cotton now stored in the States, respecting which opinions are very conflicting. Estimates of it range from two to five millions of bales. If this pours like a flood into our market, it will for a time depress prices ; but the day has gone by for America to produce cotton at 3d. to 4d. per lb' as in 1847 to 1850. That was the cause why all other producers had to succumb to her. The cost in America had been gradually but permanently rising since 1850, and I believe that prior to the outbreak of the civil war the United States could not produce good and well-cleaned cotton of the first quality under a cost of 6d. per lb. selling price. This was not generally known; other producers had been floored by the 3d. to 4d., and were afraid of a reaction to those rates again. Under no circumstances can the United States produce good cotton under 6d. per lb., and the probability is that they will not for a long time, for obvious reasons, be able to do anything under 8d. to 9d. So that, if Brazil can produce a superior quality at 5d., she has no occasion to dread fair competition in the long run ; but she and all other countries must make up their minds to face for a time, or at some time, that mass of cotton now said to be stored in the States. It really would be better, I think, to know that it was all burnt, whereas it is known that not 50,000 bales have yet been destroyed (this, by-the-by, is the reason why people are so shy of trying their hands at getting cotton from India).

Now, as to qualities and quantities, you will find the two Haytian bales adjoining the Natal Court, and especially alluded to in my Report.

First, we want 4,000,000 bales of one or both united ; now worth 16*d*. to 18*d*., usually 6*d*. to 7*d*. per lb.

Secondly, 250,000 bales of that quality or qualities known as Egyptian or Brazilian, including all classes of Brazilian. These cottons are used partly to supplement the higher grades, and in times like the present largely in substitution of the low grades forming part of the 4,000,000, because their prices are relatively cheaper than American.

Thirdly, we want 40,000 to 50,000 bales of the long Sea Island, like the bale from Queensland; worth at present about 4*s*. per lb., usually 20*d*. to 30*d*. So you will see that there is a large field open for all.

Many cultivators run away with the idea that it will be most to their interest to grow those cottons—viz., Sea Islands, because they sell the highest. This is a very delusive reason. First, the yield per acre is very much less than other varieties,—not half what New Orleans would be in weight. Secondly, it is very speculative, for it is only the best quality that sells high. The crop may be stained, and then only sells for the price of Orleans; therefore the producer may be disappointed in more ways than one. The other sorts are a more certain crop. In the United States an acre will yield a bale of 450 lb. of clean cotton. I should say, from my knowledge of Brazil, that the soil there ought to do as much if it is not robbed, *i.e.*, by carrying off from the land the plant, the cotton, and the cotton seed, and not manuring. The cotton-seed is a valuable, rich, oily manure, and if it is carried away and used for cattle food, or for extracting the oil from it, then some animal or artificial manure should be used to replace it. The yield in India is so small (not exceeding 100 lb. per acre), and the quality so poor, solely because the land has been robbed and not manured, and improperly, or not at all, ploughed; for, where the land has been ploughed, and the crop manured, the quantity and the quality have both improved wonderfully. In India we also find the natives very anxious to get hold of improved agricultural implements, ploughs, harrows, and hoes, and quite appreciating them.

Next, the mode of gathering the crop. The Americans do this systematically. As soon as any ripe bolls appear, they commence picking, and pick day by day the ripe bolls. These are stored and baled separately from the inferior and dirty. They sort their crop into three qualities, and are repaid for their trouble. In India and Smyrna the people gather the whole crop at once—the ripe and the over-ripe, and the immature bolls altogether; the consequence is that they are not repaid, for the mass of fibres, in all stages of growth, cannot be used by any machinery without great loss from the irregularity of the whole.

Next the ginning. The Americans use for the Sea Island the Macarthy gin, and all evidence goes to prove that this gin is the best, and the only gin which does not injure long staples. Those are Sea Island, Brazilian, and Egyptian; it also cleans New Orleans with less injury than the saw-gin, but does less quantity, and therefore is not in favour.

The saw-gin injures all cottons except American and African. It chops East Indian to bits. The best implement for East Indian or other short-stapled is, I think,

Platt's or Dunlop's, or Dobson and Barlow's gins; but this is a question which at present is not by any means decided. Ginning is a very important affair, for I can show cotton worth 13*d.* per lb. cleaned in a proper machine, and the same cotton, having been put through an improper machine, worth only 8*d.*

Our Association will be glad to give you a moderate supply of seeds of various varieties for the Brazilian Government; namely, Sea Island, Egyptian, and New Orleans. If the Brazilian Government require large quantities, we can indicate to you the best way of obtaining them on moderate terms. I should recommend a trial of each kind to be made in each province; that prizes should be offered for the best-prepared crops of each; that the local governments of each province should be supplied with cotton gins of various constructions, either as models for local mechanics, or on sale; for experience has proved that cotton seed supplied, without the means of ginning—*i. e.* separating the seed from the fibre—will do no good.

The local authorities ought also to be furnished with samples of the various kinds of cottons which we require; these the Cotton Supply Association will gladly furnish in such quantities as may be required.

The Brazilian Government should also provide for the means of bringing the cotton to the ports—it is a bulky article, and requires great facilities for transport. The railways now making will do much for this; but roads and tramroads will be required to feed the railways.

Cotton presses should be introduced to reduce the bulk as much as possible in the interior. I think that the foregoing embraces nearly all the points alluded to in yours; but if I have omitted any, I shall be glad to attend to them.

Believe me, &c.,

W. WANKLYN.

To JOHN MIERS, Esq

———————————

(Reply to Application for Wool Samples.)

LONDON WALL, 18th January, 1865.

SIR,—In reply to your letter of yesterday, asking us to supply you with samples of Australian and Cape Wools for exhibiting in the Dublin International Exhibition, we beg to inform you that we are not able to assist you in this matter, being merely warehouse-keepers. The brokers in the trade are the proper parties, we believe, to aid you in your requirements.

We remain, Sir,

Your obedient Servants,

GOOCH & COUSENS.

P. L. SIMMONDS, Esq.

———————————

(Report on Manure.)

8, MARKET STREET, FAVERSHAM,
December 14th, 1865.

GENTLEMEN,—Having obtained the sole agency in Kent for the sale of your "Concentrated Fæcal Manure," we have much pleasure in presenting our report.

The manure having only been introduced into this district in the spring of the present year, we had considerable difficulty in prevailing upon agriculturists generally to give it a trial, for two reasons :—

1st. That farmers are proverbially wary of anything new, and regard it more or less with suspicion.

2nd. That having been frequently imposed on by spurious and worthless compositions, under the name of artificial manures, they are consequently afraid to lay out money upon any but those kinds which have stood the test of repeated trials, and by long experience proved themselves to be good. The result has, however, far exceeded our expectations, both as to the quantity sold and the effects produced. It affords us much gratification to be able to afford you so many valuable testimonials from thoroughly practical men. We invite their careful perusal.

We may just add, we have ourselves given the manure a fair trial, with hops, corn, roots, and vegetables, and have been much pleased with the results.

We shall be happy to give particulars to any person requiring further information.

As to the mode of application, our experience and observations lead us to recommend that, where practicable, it should be *drilled* into the furrows, and if mixed with a proportion of ashes, so much the better. If sown *broadcast*, it is desirable to use it as early in the season as possible.

We are, Gentlemen,

Your obedient Servants,

THOS. & B. G. BERRY.

(Letter with Advertisement for Publication.)

MANCHESTER, *April 5th*, 1865.

Mr. JOHN FALCONER, Printer,
  Dublin.

SIR,—Enclosed we hand you our advertisement for the Dublin International Exhibition Official Catalogue, for the entire edition (viz. 40,000), which we should wish to occupy a quarter of a page. On receipt of the bill of charge for insertion from yourself or the Secretary, we will immediately forward you a P. O. O. for the amount. We should like to see a proof, if possible, when in type.

   We are, Sir,
    Yours respectfully,
     BARRIE & Co.

(Advice of Shipment of Cases, with Instructions.)

LONDON, *April 12th*, 1865.

DEAR SIR,—We yesterday afternoon delivered at the Dublin Steam Wharf, consigned to you, marked R. F., Nos. 1 and 2, Two Cases, containing Model in hard wood of the Royal Exchange, and a glazed case for its protection.

We shall be glad to hear from you that they have reached their destination safely, and shall feel obliged if you will have the model put together by competent workmen, sending us note of charges incurred.

Yours truly,

For ROBT. FAUNTLEROY & Co.,

THOMAS DAY.

P. L. SIMMONDS, Esq.

(On Jamaica Fibres.)

BATH, JAMAICA, *March 17th*, 1865.

P. L SIMMONDS, Esq.

MY DEAR SIR,—I have been very busy for the last two months, getting up a Collection of Fibres for the Dublin Exhibition, and although the time you allowed to prepare them was very limited, still I think they will be found superior. They cannot fail to attract great attention, more particularly so if they are arranged with anything like taste and order, taking care to place the textiles by themselves, and spreading out the web-like pieces. I have dyed a few to show they will take dye. I enclose a detailed list of them. You will find many detached pieces, got up with much care, for attracting the attention of the public. The whole are packed in a box a little over four feet in length by one or more in breadth, consigned to you, at 454, West Strand, in the absence of knowing the proper address. The box, I am informed, was shipped on board the Liverpool steamer *Chilian*. The Company's depôt in London is 30, Great St. Helen's. The box was put on board on the 8th inst. at Port Royal, and taken as a great favour, as the vessel refused more cargo, so that the freight was not prepaid, which I had intended; but this I will settle with you when I know the amount.

I wish it to be well understood, that at the close of the Exhibition these fibres are to be considered your private property, and under these conditions will be exhibited; and I do hope that you will not allow them to be indiscriminately dispersed, as those I sent in 1862 were. These fibres represent in a small degree the wealth of the island and its applicability to industrial pursuits, and more particularly the rank and profuse vegetation we are favoured with; but without machinery these can be of no avail in a commercial point of view. It will be useless for any person to apply to me for a supply or to know how such can be obtained; by the aid of machinery and English capital, however, much might be done.

Let me know what I owe you for books, and write me when you receive the box containing the fibres.

I am, Dear Sir,

Yours truly,

N. WILSON.

(The same.)

BATH, JAMAICA, 7th October, 1865.

P. L. SIMMONDS, Esq.

DEAR SIR,—I am glad to hear you have received my fibres and approve of them, and that they were generally admired in the Dublin Exhibition; I only wish they could be made useful commercially. Although the three

collections I have sent to these Great Exhibitions have
been admitted to be very superior, still it is to be
regretted that they still rank among our waste products,
with the exception of the bamboo, which the Americans
are now making good use of for news printing-paper, &c.   I
wish you could induce some of your monied firms, or fibre
brokers, to send out some efficient, simple, and cheap
machinery for cleaning the fibre of the herbaceous plants ;
such as pinguins, plantains, or bananas.   The annual
waste of these is very great, and without machinery will
never be available ; more particularly so as we have such
an indolent population to deal with, who allow the island to
go headlong to destruction, and are every day becoming
worse, while fine land is almost unsaleable, so that it
would not cost much to establish a fibre manufactory
here.

I am glad to hear your determination not to let my
collection of fibres slip through your hands this time.
No doubt the distribution of prizes will soon take place,
and I trust my contribution will be deemed worth notice.

It is with much pleasure I inform you that one of
the Cinchona trees imported (*C. succirubra*) is now in
flower at an altitude of 5,000 feet, at the foot of
Catherine Peak, where it is always cool and moist, and the
richest district we have for rare ferns. If your friends have
still a mania for growing them, I can supply them at
£10 per case, exclusive of freight, by appointing an agent
in Kingston to ship them.

I have been told the bamboo yields 70 per cent. fibre,
and by personal observation I have ascertained that it
attains its full height of 90 or 100 feet in the short space

of four or five months, growing at the average rate of eight inches in twenty-four hours. Those in my collection were taken when in a young growing state, and not more than twenty or thirty feet in height.

There is another great International Exhibition now open in Erfurt, Prussia, and I was called upon by the consul here to contribute a collection of fibres to it, which I have done, and I naturally surmise that some good to the island ought to be the result. Try what you can do through the all-powerful press.

Yours truly,

N. WILSON.

(On Ceylon Fibres and Paper Material.)

BADULLA, 26th April, 1866.

DEAR SIR,—I had the pleasure of receiving your favour of the 26th February on the 29th March last. and I am very much obliged to you for all the information you kindly promise to procure for me.

By this mail I send you a catalogue of the natural and artificial products of Ceylon, intended to represent the industry and resources of the colony at the Paris Exhibition.

A week ago I had the satisfaction of showing the vegetable products, collected and prepared by me, to the Lieut.-Governor of Ceylon, and I brought to his notice that it would be very desirable to send them to England for the information of traders and merchants. He readily promised me to send a small box, so I have some hopes of forwarding you a number of useful specimens.

I am at present engaged in preparing my paper-pulp (of which I have already written to you) for the Chamber of Commerce at Colombo, who have agreed to take five tons of it at $1\frac{1}{2}d$. per lb.

As far as I have had the means of testing this new material for paper, I am inclined to think that it will produce an excellent smooth durable substance. The tree from which the bark is extracted grows in abundance in the district of Ouvah, and the pulp may be prepared at a low rate. I am anxious to have this new material, prepared from the bark of the *Gnidia eriocephala*, duly *registered* in the records of the Society of Arts, to enable me hereafter to apply for a patent should the article become one of commercial importance. If you would kindly comply with this request, you would confer a favour on me, which will be duly appreciated.

Hitherto I have only extracted the *Sanseviera* fibre by hand, and find it could never be remunerating by this method, as a man can only clean half a pound per diem, and his labour costs $7\frac{1}{2}d$.

If you could oblige me with a drawing or small model of Mr. Burke's fibre-cleaning machine, I should like to try it for preparing this most important and valuable fibre.

Hoping to be favoured with your communication,

I remain, dear Sir,

Yours sincerely,

WM. C. ONDAATJE.

P. L. SIMMONDS, Esq., London.

(Letter on the Fibres of Commerce.)

BASINGHALL STREET, E.C.

P. L. SIMMONDS, Esq., F.S.S.

SIR,—I have long been accustomed to look out for the *Technologist* to bring me information of what transpires having relation to industrial subjects only otherwise found by diffused and almost random reading. But it has continually struck me that some of the information would be greatly increased in value if given less in the abstract— a manner of presenting information calculated frequently to mislead, and to foster erroneous ideas in the minds of even some practical men.

Again, suggestive information is greatly needed by men whose labours lie in applying science on some subjects which seem to make absolutely *no* progress;— doubtless, because authorities are so very rare and scanty to which to turn for the *minute* information which science alone can eliminate, and upon which must be built up all improvement.

During fifteen years of practical study of *fibres*, I have found this dearth a serious hindrance, having literally to weed out a thousand loose conclusions given as authorities of high standing, all leading in a wrong direction, before finding one sufficiently reliable on which safely to base action. In one important process on animal fibres, I believe I have recently succeeded in fully setting the subject at rest ; or, at least, in furnishing a solid corner-stone on which the future may build. My present labours lie among vegetable fibres suitable for textile fabrics. Here, all is at a standstill. Despite the multitude of

C

fibres brought under notice during many years past, and notwithstanding the high value of the fibres now in use, the subject will, doubtless, remain at a standstill until the manufacturers have new fibrous materials exhibited to them, ready prepared in a suitable state for producing fabrics possessing some excellencies or beauties peculiar to themselves.

Towards progress in this direction my slight aid is forthcoming, and it would be a public boon if there were brought before men engaged in such research the peculiar properties of various fibres with corrections of false notions concerning them. Such information might, at least, do much to rescue the age from the charlatanism palmed upon it by ignorance, clothed in patent rights of old parchment value. If you can furnish such aid, it will be exceedingly welcome, and will, doubtless, call forth others. Whilst confessedly wishful to occupy the place of a student, I should also be glad to endeavour to clear up a little of the dimness on the subject (by reference to facts which have developed themselves under my notice), and thus call out further light on these matters, which may be practically useful.

Yours very respectfully,

J. SMITH.

(Proposal to Establish a Shoddy Factory.)

4, SKINNER'S PLACE, SISE LANE.

P. L. SIMMONDS, Esq.

DEAR SIR,—The demand for Wool being considerably in excess of the supply, many projects have been and are being tried to make good the deficiency; and several inventions are at work in England to effect this purpose, all more or less attended with success, according to the perfection to which the mechanical and chemical processes have been brought.

The price of half woollen rags in England is from £8 to £10 per ton, and leaves a good profit on the extraction of the Wool even when all else is wasted; and recently a Limited Liability Company, with £150,000 Capital, has been promoted for carrying out a patent in England.

In France, where the supply of rags is as great as in England, there is no beneficial system of converting them into Wool, and they are used for manure. The well-known rag export duty prevents their transmission to England.

It is therefore proposed to establish, near Paris, a factory for the introduction of this branch of business, and working a recently-secured French patent, of great value, but of the simplest and most practical character, by which all the Wool can be extracted from rags in a pure, unburnt condition, and the carbon produced from the vegetable portion of the rags, preserved, for which there is a ready market for sanitary and agricultural purposes.

Suitable premises near Paris can now be obtained, with a good water supply, which is very important.

It is proposed to commence on a small scale, and convert about a ton of rags per day; and after the whole has been at work sufficient time the operations may be extended, or the plant, works, &c., sold to a large Public Company.

The income for one year would be as follows :—

156 Tons of Wool, at £37 ....£5,772		
78 „ Carbon, at £6 468		
		6,240

At a cost for machinery, plant, fixing,
&c., capable of working one ton of
rags per day, about £1,230
Six months' working expenses, including
cost of rags, wages, materials, and
every other expense, about 1,760

  ——— 2,990

Leaving a Profit of £3,250

The owners of the patents, &c., desire to meet with a capitalist who will invest £4,000 in the above business, on the terms of equal Shares in everything that can be produced, either by the working or sale of the inventions, &c.

Yours truly,

SANDELL & MADDERS.

(Advising Improved Process of Preparing Fibres.)

80, LOMBARD STREET, LONDON.

SIR,—An invention has recently been patented for "Improvements in Treating Flax, Hemp, and other Fibrous Matters requiring like treatment."

This invention, secured under Letters Patent, granted to Messrs. Burton and Pye, is now vested solely in us.

Its specific objects are the preparation of Flax and

other similar fibres, without the steeping or retting process hitherto in use. By machinery of a simple character, a speedy, uniform, and economical mode of treatment is substituted for a tedious, uncertain, and costly one, and by the application of fuller's earth in solution, in combination with steam and alternating pressure, the fibre is effectually cleansed from the gluten and other impurities so difficult of removal by the present systems, and presented—ready for use—in a shorter time, with less waste, and in a much better condition for the subsequent processes, than has ever yet been accomplished.

Another important feature in this invention is, that the boon or woody portion of the plant, which has hitherto been destroyed, is so preserved as to be easily converted into meal or flour, of great value as food for cattle.

It is scarcely possible to exaggerate the important influence which the adoption of this principle may exercise on the future production of Flax; thus rendering the subject one of very deep interest to all concerned in its growth as well as its manufacture.

Influenced by these convictions, we have established a House under the firm of Pye Brothers, with the object of fully developing the character and advantages of this invention, the value of which, in a national point of view, the Royal Agricultural Societies of England and of Ireland have already recognized by awards of first-class prizes.

The machines used in the several processes may be seen in operation at our Grey-Friars Works, Ipswich.

Applications for viewing them, and for all other information relative to their nature, cost, and results, and for the transaction of all business connected with the invention, may be addressed to,

Sir,

Your obedient Servants,

PYE BROTHERS.

January, 1857.

(Advising Shipment of Earthenware to Portugal.)

BURSLEM, *August 5th*, 1865.

P. L. SIMMONDS, Esq., London.

DEAR SIR,—Your favour of the 4th inst. is to hand. In reply, we beg to say that we have sent, through the agency of Mr. Charles Botterill, Liverpool, to be forwarded to our friend, Mr. Augustus J. Shore, Oporto, a cask of samples of earthenware, weighing,

Gross .... 1 cwt. 3 qr. 20 lb.

Nett............... 1 cwt. 0 qr. 7 lb.

We will send you detailed particulars of this package by an early post.

Remaining, dear Sir,

Yours respectfully,

Pro HOPE & CARTER,

J. ROCK.

August, 1865.

Messrs. ROBINSON & Co., City.

GENTLEMEN,—I am in receipt of yours of yesterday, and take note of sales advised. I am aware I have received

£150 on account of consignments, and my only motive for asking you for account sales was to get them passed through the books. You have still on hand for me unaccounted as yet, besides these Bombay shipments :

1865.

March 8—2 cases, per *W. Simpson*, to Japan	£35 12	6
„ 1 case, per *Vicar of Bray*, to Lima	20 17	0

1865.

February 23—1 case, per *Calderon*, to Madras	33 12	6
March 22—2 cases, per *Calcutta*, to Colombo	34 11	0

of which I shall be glad to hear when you receive advices.

I remain, yours truly,
THOMAS MITCHELL.

(Order to Broker.)

BOND STREET.

Mr. JENKINSON, Mincing-lane.

DEAR SIR,—Please buy for me 1 case oil citronella, good quality, and 5 cwt. almond oil.

I suppose I may give up all hope of getting the cask of naphtha ordered from you two months ago.

Yours truly,
EDWARD PHILLIPS.

(Advising Forwarding Samples.)

LONDON, *April 3rd*, 1866.

P. L. SIMMONDS, Esq.

MY DEAR SIR,—In accordance with the wish expressed in your note of yesterday, we shall send by messenger to-morrow to John Street, Adelphi, addressed to you, a box containing the specimens that you name, to illustrate the lecture on sugar-refining, &c., and which we trust will be found suitable.   They will consist of as below named.

Yours truly,

L. COWAN & SONS.

No. 1.—Bones.

    2.—Carbonized bones; viz., bones burnt in airtight retorts.

    3.—Ditto ground into grain, known as " Animal Charcoal," through which the liquid, or diluted sugar, passes to become decolourized.

    4.—Sugar as imported.

    5.—Ditto diluted and made ready to be passed through the charcoal.

    6.—The diluted sugar after having passed through the charcoal.

    7.—Ditto after having been boiled in a vacuum-pan and dried in a centrifugal machine, known as " refined sugar."

Messrs. GREENSLADE & Co.

GENTLEMEN,—As there was no agreement made respecting the deduction for the case when the order was given, I will allow in this instance the 6*s.* ; but in future I cannot do so, as it is quite contrary to my usual practice to allow for cases.

Your obedient Servant,

S. ROTE.

(Inquiry as to Responsibility.)

LONDON, *July*, 1866.

GENTLEMEN,—Would you kindly furnish us with what information you may possess as to the standing and responsibility of Messrs. Bull & Co., Nelson, New Zealand, who desire to enter into business relations with us, and have requested us to apply to you for references ?

We have the honour to be, Gentlemen,

Your obedient Servants,

SMITH, STEVENS, & Co.

(Letter of Inquiry from a Colonial Merchant.)

PORT ELIZABETH, 22*nd January*, 1866.

P. L. SIMMONDS, Esq.

DEAR SIR,—Can you furnish me with a good receipt for anti-friction grease ? I have had one sent from England consisting of $\frac{3}{4}$ cwt. grey lime, $\frac{1}{2}$ cwt. oil, 50 gallons water to the lime.

The instructions for manipulating are not clear; but apart from that it is evidently not the A. F. G. I want, as the A. F. G. imported here smells strongly of *tar*, or some of its products, and the above would not do so unless the oil used is meant to be a mineral oil.

The anti-friction grease imported into this colony acts as a blister, and is used as such for horses, &c. Is this owing to the causticity of the lime, or to any other ingredient?

There is in this colony unfortunately a dearth of all manufactures—even soap is comparatively neglected, as the uncertainty of supplies of tallow is great, and of oil only a very small quantity of linseed is manufactured in Cape Town.

Trusting that this communication may not be deemed either impertinent or trivial, I beg to subscribe myself, Sir,

Yours sincerely,
OCTAVIUS CRAWFORD.

(Reply to Claim for Deductions.)

3rd July.

Messrs. CHANDLER & CO.

GENTLEMEN,—As you do not consider my proposal a just one, I beg to inform you that, to save both of us troublesome correspondence, I agree to make the allowances you require, but with the small alterations as under.

1. Your invoice is in francs, and of course I cannot allow you the deduction in shillings.

Annexed I enclose you the copy of the claim amended as per my books, and I hope you will find it correct.

Your early reply will oblige.

PHILIP MATHESON.

124	$\frac{1}{12}$ doz.	at fr.	3 50	...... Fr.	0 27
.,	$\frac{1}{4}$ "		6	......	1 50
126	$\frac{1}{4}$ "		9	......	2 25
3	$\frac{1}{3}$ "		6	......	2 0
5	$\frac{1}{12}$ "		12	......	1 0
108	$\frac{1}{12}$ "		6	......	0 50
53	1.		24	......	24 0

Fr. 31 52

Less 15 % discount 4 72

26 80

Transport 9 40

Fr. 36 20

or £1. 9s. 3d.

(Inquiry as to the Commercial Value of Tasmanian Barks.)

VAN DIEMEN'S LAND COMPANY OFFICES,
6, GREAT WINCHESTER STREET, E.C.,
6th January, 1863.

SIR,—The Directors of this Company have received from the colony certain specimens of sassafras and (so called) myrtle bark, the latter a species of beech; and we are desirous of ascertaining whether both or either of them possess qualities to render them valuable in the arts of medicine, dyeing, &c., or otherwise.

At the suggestion of their friend Mr. Youl, they take the liberty of sending you portions of the bark for your inspection, and would be greatly obliged if you could ascertain for their information the points in question, and favour them with the result.

I am, your obedient Servant,

H. CATTLEY, Secretary.

P.S.—Sent per Parcels Delivery Company.

To P. L. SIMMONDS, Esq.

(Reply to Proposals of an Agency Company.)

24th January, 1863.

DEAR SIR,—Your note of the 22nd inst. reached me yesterday. I have no doubt that, properly managed, a small number of Russian producers may avail themselves of the conveniences and facilities your Company offers. But I cannot bring this matter before the Russian public by inserting the Company's propositions in my official report, or by publishing the same separately, without having explanations on several special points; namely : First, will goods require to be put in glass cases, or other expensive contrivances, for their proper exhibition ; if so, at what rates will the exhibitors be charged with these expenses ?

Secondly, it would be better to have an exact statement of the amount of reduction in the expenses for taking out patents ; and, concerning infringements of patent rights, the producers or exhibitors will ask, in what proportion to the value or price of their exhibited goods the Company will limit its advances, and in what manner will the Company be answerable for the loyal conduct of the legal proceedings against infringements of patent rights ?

The fourth point promises more than can be performed ; at least this will be the opinion of foreign producers and commercial men.

Concerning the commission for sales effected by the Company's officers, the rate of charge is not stated in figures. Foreign producers do not know what in this respect is usual in London. Such knowledge is limited to the exporting commercial houses.

I felt it my duty to submit to you these cursory remarks, because in relation to foreigners, and particularly to people of the eastern part of Europe, much depends upon the plain clearness and comprehensiveness of each point of your Company's programme.

Should you like to communicate to me explanations, I will be glad to make them known through several of the Russian special newspapers and reviews. My address in St. Petersburg is, Scientific Committee of the Ministry of Crown Domains.

I hope to have the pleasure to meet you before I leave England, at the end of this month.

Believe me, truly yours,

GEORGE KASPARSON.

P. L. SIMMONDS, Esq.

(Agreeing to Supply Goods.)

LONDON, July 9th, 1865.

Mr. MITCHELSON, Sunderland.

DEAR SIR,—Your letter of the 4th is to hand, and I beg to inform you that I shall be very happy to supply you with the articles named, at the prices as per enclosed list, upon the following terms :—Cash in advance first transaction.   Three months' account, 5 per cent. discount, with satisfactory references in London, or for cash, 7½ per cent. discount.

Yours truly,
SIMON PICKSLEY.

(Instructions for Purchase, &c. to Colonial Brokers.)

Messrs. ELLIS & HALE,
    Lime Street.

DEAR SIRS,—Please buy for me the caddy of musk which I inspected yesterday, at 20s. 6d. per oz., and the case of Mexican vanilla at 30s. per lb., and if you will please clear them for me I will send to your office for them on Thursday.

I sent this morning to Scott's Wharf for the pipe of olive oil, and to my great disappointment they sent back the carman without it; first, because it had not been re-gauged to you; and, second, because they said it wanted a stamp at the back of the order. Now, there is already one on front of the Delivery Order, on which is the signature "E. Stone & Co.," and I never knew it required two stamps to one order.   The Japan wax and oil of bays had no stamp, and yet no difficulty was made.

Please tell me if they were right in refusing to deliver the oil; if not, they certainly ought to pay the extra cartage—viz., 4s. 6d.

Yours truly,
N. BERRY.

(Inquiry as to Responsibility.)

Messrs. BATEMAN & ROSS.

GENTLEMEN,—You will oblige me by stating if Mr. H. Perkins, of Long Row, Leicester, is known to you and worthy of credit.

I am, Gentlemen,
Your obedient Servant,
W. ATHERTON.

(Inviting Tenders for Work.)

STRAND.

Messrs. BODYS & REID.

GENTLEMEN,—We have decided on dividing the work to be done into three distinct contracts, viz. :—

1. Putting up large steam boiler with smoke-consuming apparatus, erecting two extra open pans, and girding the whole with iron, and fitting up drying-room.

2. Replacing the stoves in shop with steam pipes connected with the boiler below, allowing for price of stoves.

3. Fitting up the boiler up-stairs with smoke-consuming apparatus; that for both boilers to be guaranteed.

Please send me, per return, a separate estimate for each job, and oblige

Your obedient Servants,
JOHNSON & Co.

(Letter to Printers.)

Messrs. McGOWAN & DANKS,
    Printers.

GENTLEMEN,—If I do not receive by Monday 50,000 of
the English bills, 12,500 Portuguese, and 12,500 Spanish,
you can consider the first part of my order cancelled.
Do not send less than the above quantities.

It is strange that while you promise the completion of
work by a certain date, you never fulfil your promises.

             Yours truly,
                PHILIP LUND.

(West African Trade.)

             LAGOS, *20th October*, 1865.

Mr. JOHN WITHAMS,
    River Nun.

DEAR SIR,—The *Cecil* leaves to-day, and by her I
send you two casks of rice, one case of preserved meats,
cask of yams, guinea fowl, fowls, sheep and goats, which
I trust will reach you safely. You will see on the back
of the B. L. what I have taken out of the *Cecil*. You
can land the remainder with the exception of the crane,
which I have been unable to land.

I wish you to be very careful and particular when
landing the rum ; have each cask opened before it leaves
the ship, and ascertain if any and how much has been
taken out. If you find the rum short, advise our agent.
You will see by the invoice I sent you how much rum
each cask should contain. If you do not require all the

tenter-hooks send me the half (5,000) back. I trust you
have lots of oil, much more than will ballast the *Cecil*.
Do not keep her one day more than you can help, and
use every exertion to discharge and load her up here.

No appearance of the *St. Lawrence* yet ! On what day
did she leave ? Send me the certificate of her "lay days"
at the Nun. I hope to hear from you fully by mail.

JOHN HILDEBRAND,
Agent West African Company (Limited).

LAGOS, *September*, 1865.

DEAR SIR,—I take the opportunity of the *Investigator*
going up the Niger to inform you that the *Manchester*
will leave here for the Nun in a couple of days, so that
you may be ready for her when she arrives. I have
taken out of her the salt and a few of the " packs," the
exact quantity of which you will find endorsed on the
back of captain's bill of lading.

I send copy of the invoices, that you may see what the
different goods cost in England. Despatch the *Manchester* as quick as possible, as I have cargo here waiting
for her. I hope you have a considerable quantity of oil
ready for her. Let me know what you are in want of,
and if any provisions arrive, I will try and send you
some.

Trusting you are in the best of health,

I am, dear Sir,
Yours truly,

E. GOODWIN, Esq.   FRED. LAWRENCE.

LAGOS, *November 20th*, 1865.

C. COOLEY, Esq., Calabar River.

DEAR SIR,—I am unable this week to send any one to relieve you, but have made arrangements to do so next month.

The *Cecil* has, I hope, long ago left with everything you had to ship safely on board. Should she, by some unforeseen accident, still be in the river, send up by her 700 cases of the gin you have in stock. The *Manchester* sailed for Liverpool this morning with a full cargo, a good part our own. The *St. Lawrence* is still outside, hands all sick and unable to take more than a boat-load of oil a day, although I have sent six more hands on board to stow. I send you by the mail some blank bills of lading. I hope you keep in good health, and am

Yours truly,

JOHN HILDEBRAND.

———

LAGOS, *10th August*, 1865.

Mr. BROWNE.

DEAR SIR,—I send Mr. Paterson to relieve you, so that you may come on by the return mail steamer. You will have again to take stock carefully, without however opening the casks containing the powder. The powder in the store can be counted if any has been sold, or if Mr. Paterson wishes it. He must sign the stock-sheet, a copy of which you will leave with him. The quantity of palm-oil you have on board must be stated on the stock-sheet. See the wood of the Iron house properly stowed and protected from the weather before you leave, if not already done. Put Mr. Paterson up to the character of the natives and others with whom he will be brought in contact. Show him what you have been paying for oil, and the way to ascertain contents of casks as distinguished from gauges. I send the sheets on which the oil account appears to have been kept from the establishment of the factory till June 16, 1865. Will you make them up to the time you leave? I suppose you can also give me all the shipments that have been made from the factory.

Yours truly,

B. WOOLHOUSE.

(Letters regarding Settlement of Claims for Sea-damaged Sugar.)

HAVRE, 4th March, 1864.

Mr. P. L. SIMMONDS, London.

DEAR SIR,—I duly received your letter of the 28th April, and with all my pushing could not get the *procès verbal* from our Tribunal of Commerce before yesterday afternoon. They have, by law, 20 days' time after the sale, and as there have been a great many public sales lately, I could not obtain greater despatch. All the documents go to London to-night.

The sale produced 52,691 francs; the charges amount to 1,070 francs 90 centimes. The value of the sugar in sound state is on the basis of 41 francs the No. 12.

Frs. 43.25 for STB, 94 cases	......	4,065	50
„ 43 „ STA, 38 „	......	1,634	
„ 41.75 „ ST, 247 „	......	10,312	25
		16,011	75

I remain, Sir,
Yours truly,
For Edw. Andreae,

P. GREVE.

HAVRE, 23rd *April*, 1864.

Mr. P. L. SIMMONDS, London.

DEAR SIR,—In reply to your letter of the 19th I have until this day been unable to terminate the affair *Minerva*, but hope to send you all particulars by next Monday evening's mail.

I remain, Dear Sir,

Yours truly,

For Edw. Andreae,

P. GREVE.

"THE OCEAN" MARINE INSURANCE COMPANY,

2, OLD BROAD STREET,

LONDON, E.C., 8th *June*, 1864.

P. L. SIMMONDS, Esq. London.

SIR,—We, the undersigned Underwriters on a cargo of sugar, per *Timandra*, @ Havana, arrived at Hamburg, request you to proceed thither forthwith, and hereby authorize you to arrange the settlement for particular average with the consignees of the cargo as you may deem fit. We hereby agree to contribute our respective proportions of any expenses so incurred.

For the Ocean Marine Insurance Company,

FREDERICK HARFORD,

M. HAMMOND, for self.

&c., &c.

"THE OCEAN" MARINE INSURANCE COMPANY,
2, OLD BROAD STREET,
LONDON, E.C., *8th June*, 1864.

Timandra.

DEAR SIR,—With reference to the particulars of cargo
by the above vessel, the declaration on our own and other
policies is upon

T.F. $^{1}/_{2248}$. 2248 boxes sugar, valued at £13,000.

I am, dear Sir,
Yours truly,
H. S. SMYTH, Secretary.

P. L. SIMMONDS, Esq.

HAMBURG, *11th June*, 1864.

DEAR SIR,—I have to report to you that I arrived at
Hamburg yesterday, and immediately placed myself in
communication with Lloyd's agent, and obtained the
particulars of the official survey which had been made;
to-day, with an experienced broker who had been called
in to value the damaged sugar, I carefully examined the
boxes, which are deposited in two different warehouses,
and herewith I append an estimate of damage, which is
certainly very heavy. Apparently, from .the captain's
report, the vessel shipped heavy seas during a great part
of her voyage, and hence the extensive loss and damage.
I endeavoured to effect a compromise by making a *pro rata*
allowance to the owners, but they were unwilling to negotiate, and preferred to relinquish to the underwriters as

a total loss. As prices come better from Mincing-lane, and there seems an upward tendency in the produce-markets here, I hope at the public sale, to which I fear I shall have to resort, something like fair prices may be realized. Unfortunately the local demand is not great here, there being but two refineries, which appear to be well stocked, and the publicity that can be given will not be sufficient to draw buyers from distant parts. Unfortunately the longer the sale is delayed the greater will be the deficiency in weight by drainage. I have hopes that I may yet save the expenses of public sale, having had a private offer for the whole, the only question in dispute being, how much allowance shall be made, the bidder wishing for an abatement of four marks per 100 lb., while I consider three is a sufficient deduction.

I am, dear Sir,

Yours truly,

P. L. SIMMONDS.

P.S.—After due consideration and much dispute, I accepted the offer for the whole of the sugar, allowing an abatement of 3 marks 8 on the sound value, leaving Lloyd's agent to see to the delivery and settlement.

TIMANDRA.

Approximate Estimate of Damage.

1917 boxes damaged.

99 „ all empty.

and 7 casks molasses, &c., filled up.

———

2016 boxes.

2016 boxes should weigh at about 360lb.
each..................................... Net 690,120 lb.

According to calculation,
99 empty boxes at
about 360 lb. each ... Net   35,640 lb.

300 half or more empty
boxes, at 180 lb. each,
(average) .... Net   54,000 lb.

1617 boxes more or less
damaged, at 320 lb.
each (purposely rather
high allowance) ...... Net 517,440 lb.

                                        Net 607,080 lb.

Probable loss on weight about .... Net 83,040 lb.

At valued price of 24 Mk. 8s. bco. per
100 lb...................................... Rtlr. 20,335
      (or £1534 14 4)

Allowance on 1,917 boxes, weighing
571,440 lb., at 4 Mk. bco. per 100 lb. ... Rtlr. 22,857

                                       £3,259 15 6

4 Mk. allowance, equal to 16¼ per cent. on sound value
                                of the sugar.

3 „   8s. „   „   14¼   „   „
3 „   „   „   12½   „   „
2 „   8s. „   „   10⅕   „   „

LONDON, *July 14th*, 1863.

HENRY THOMPSON, Esq.

DEAR SIR,—In accordance with your letter of the 10th inst., signed also by the other underwriters, of a cargo of 2,492 boxes of sugar, per *Flamingo*, from Havannah, I proceeded the same evening to Antwerp, and on the 11th examined in the warehouses there the 729 boxes set aside as damaged, and which were all still open. These 729 boxes had been agreed as damaged by sea-water, by Mr. Jollie, Lloyd's agent, out of 1,200 originally alleged to be so damaged. About some few there might be doubt as to the cause of damage ; the great bulk were, however, unmistakeably sea-damaged, many very badly, and two boxes were empty, evidently also by the action of sea-water. The official survey having been held previously to my arrival, I did not attempt to alter it.

Next to the decision what cases are damaged, the most important proceeding is the fixing the sound value ; the two important points being to ascertain that the samples fairly represent the sound sugar, and that the standard numbers and prices are made properly. In this case there were three samples, one of 500 boxes, another of 500 boxes, and one of 1,492 boxes. The first parcel only is the property of the consignees, the second parcel belonged to an Antwerp sugar-refiner, and the 1,492 boxes were consigned for account of a house at another port ; and on this latter ground the consignees from the first declined to make a private settlement of the claim ; and though I remained at Antwerp till the afternoon of

Monday, the 13th, and went with Mr. Jollie to the refinery and to the counting-house of the consignees, making them a positive offer of a lump sum, they declared themselves unable to settle for the whole privately. It was, therefore, the more important that, on the 11th, I was present and assisted at the fixing by the brokers of the sound values of the three samples which I have with me. I saw the standard numbers of all of them on this occasion properly fixed, and this was further confirmed by the invoice numbers which I afterwards examined, and which were higher than the numbers fixed at Antwerp. The consignees, when informed of the result, expressed themselves not content therewith; but I informed Mr. Jollie that the underwriters would not consent to any modification of them. Judging from the prices paid at a sale of another parcel of damaged sugar, at which I was present, the prices of the day were also correctly fixed. I was further satisfied that in the case of the two parcels of 500 boxes each, the samples rightly represented the sugar as I inspected it at the warehouse. From the great variety in the quality of the 1,492 boxes, I was not certain that the sample exactly represented them. I therefore instructed Mr. Simpson to have a fresh sample taken of this parcel, which he will forward to me in London.

If, therefore, you should now decide to allow the sale to proceed, I shall be able to a great extent to examine the claim when it comes forward.

I am, dear Sir,

Faithfully yours,

S. Lucy.

ANTWERP, 15*th July*, 1863.

S. LUCY, Esq., London.

MY DEAR SIR,—At the close of 'Change yesterday I received a telegram from the Insurance Company authorizing me to proceed with the public sale of the 729 boxes damaged sugar, ex *Flamingo,* and I in consequence took immediate measures to have the sale announced for Saturday next, the 18th July. To-day we have advices from Holland of the Trading Company's Sugar Sale, which is reported to have gone off with much spirit, and at an advance of $1\frac{1}{2}$f. to $1\frac{3}{4}$f. per m. kilo. on the taxed prices. To-day's letters from Mincing Lane also announce a decided improvement in the demand there, and that a large business would have been done had holders not advanced their previous asking prices. These combined advices have made the Messrs. Groser very fidgety about the prospect for the sale on Saturday. As in the anticipation that an advance in prices will, by that time, be established here as elsewhere, they consider their interests will be compromised in that case, unless a fresh valuation of the sound prices of their sugars be made and admitted on that day. You will recollect that I expressed my opinion of their right to require such a re-valuation on the day of real sale, should prices of sugars advance, and that, as it would affect equally the value of the damaged as of the sound, it could not alter the loss falling on the underwriters.

Notwithstanding my having this decided opinion on their right to claim a new valuation under the circumstances anticipated by the parties, I have declined expressing it when appealed to, but shall, if need be, recognize the fresh valuation, if I see that the real position of the market sanctions any change.

Messrs. Groser continue to decline the responsibility of settling by a private arrangement their claims on the underwriters for the lot of 470 boxes damaged, lots 20 to 92, in the catalogue you have, they being a "consignment;" but to-day they were most anxious that I should compromise with them for their claims on the 259 boxes out of the two other lots, which are their own property.

After what passed with you, I should not have considered myself as authorized to repeat your offer for a compromise for the three lots, much less can I take upon myself the responsibility of negotiating for a partial settlement in the two small lots. Otherwise I feel pretty sure I could have negotiated such an arrangement for the 259 boxes on terms decidedly more favourable for the underwriters interested in them than will follow the result of the public sale.

I consider them rather less depreciated than were the 470 boxes. Your offer for the allowance on the 729 boxes was £220, which is calculated to be equal to 7 per cent. Without coming to closer quarters in the negotiation, I can only guess the terms on which I could compromise for the claims on the 270 boxes; but from what passed to-day between us, I think it probable I could arrange it by making an allowance of 10s. per box, being only 5¼ per cent., calculated at the sound price per 50 kilos, at which price each lot was valued, whereas the smallest loss resulting from a public sale would be 9 per cent., and it may be 1 to 2 per cent. more.

Will you see the underwriters immediately on the receipt of the present, and should they authorize me to negotiate such an arrangement, ask them to inform me of their decision by telegram, to be with me, if possible, to-morrow before 2 P.M.

I have had fresh samples drawn by my warehouseman from the 470 boxes, and find no appreciable difference from those I left with you.

I hope you reached your home yesterday morning comfortably, and found them all well.

I remain, my dear Sir,
Yours faithfully,
J. VANDERBILT.

ANTWERP, 17th July, 1860.

S. LUCY, Esq., London.

MY DEAR SIR,—Your favour of yesterday has just come to hand, and before the close of the Exchange yesterday I was put into possession of the telegram authorizing me to make any private settlement for the claims on the damaged sugars per *Flamingo*, I considered best for the interest of the underwriters.

Believe me, I highly appreciate this mark of confidence, and you may judge how disappointed I was when, in putting myself into communication with Messrs. Groser, I found them no longer disposed to carry through with me the negotiation spontaneously proposed to me by them on Wednesday. The only plausible reason they put forward for this change in their disposition was their having, in the intervening short interval, received advices from your city of a cargo of 1,900 boxes of sugar having been bought afloat for their account. After what had passed on the previous day between us, I could not admit of this being a justification for the false position they thereby placed me in with the underwriters ; but as there existed no explicit engagement on their part to fulfil what they led me to expect they were prepared to do, I could only express my disappointment that they should have sanctioned the communication I made to you.

For the good and better qualities of Havana sugars there is undoubtedly a somewhat better feeling amongst buyers than there was when you were here, and a sale of crushed sugar has been made to-day $\frac{3}{8}$ florin=6d. per cwt. better than was offered last week, and I foresee that Messrs. Groser will attempt to induce the brokers to make an amended valuation to-morrow, as they have to-day an urgent letter from Messrs. Murieta, calling on them to take care that the interests of the owners of the sugar to be offered to-morrow are not injured by the sale of last Saturday having been delayed.

I shall, if possible, prevent any change of price being declared ; but if I cannot succeed, I shall see that the two valuations are declared in the *procès* verbal.

I am ever, my dear Sir,
Yours very truly,
J. VANDERBILT.

ANTWERP, 18th July, 1860.

S. LUCY, Esq., London.

MY DEAR SIR,—I had this pleasure yesterday, and am now in receipt of your favour of the same date. As I

think it may be a satisfaction to your friend to hear
what passed at the sugar sale to-day, I communicate to
you the details. At the meeting of the brokers previous
to the sale, where I was present, they were unanimous
in the opinion that the transactions here during the
week required their making revised valuations, and the
result was an advance of $\frac{3}{4}$ franc per 50 kilo., about
$7\frac{1}{2}$d. per cwt. in the whole, making

Series 1, francs 30$\frac{1}{2}$ per 50 k.

       ,,   2,   ,,   33$\frac{1}{4}$,,

       ,,   3,   ,,   33$\frac{3}{4}$,,

It was decided by me, and acceded to, that the two
valuations should be inserted in the *procès verbal*, with
the reasons in support of the advance. The biddings at
the sale were animated, and there was a better disposition
to buy than I should have expected to see last Saturday.
132 Boxes, No. 1, went from 26f. to 28$\frac{1}{2}$f. average 27f.
470 ,, ,, 2,   ,,   27$\frac{1}{4}$f. to 31$\frac{1}{4}$f.   ,,   28$\frac{3}{4}$f.
127 ,, ,, 3,   ,,   29$\frac{1}{4}$f. to 34f.   ,,   31$\frac{1}{4}$f.

Of No. 1, I think there will be found 22 boxes which
sold too high to admit of a claim, and in No. 3, 43
boxes.

The No. 2 all sold, relatively to quality, the most
unfavourably, which arose from the great difference in
quality, ranging, as you may recollect from the invoice,
from Nos. 12$\frac{1}{2}$ to 19$\frac{1}{2}$ Dutch type, and the series being
arranged by the landing numbers, there was in most of
the lots a great diversity of quality, which made them
unsaleable for the manufacturers of candies, besides their
being, as I stated yesterday, more seriously sea-damaged
than Nos. 1 and 2.

Seeing the result of the sale of the two latter, and should my expectations of 65 boxes leaving no basis for claim on the underwriters prove correct, Messrs. Groser have, I think, no reason to congratulate themselves on their not having compromised their claims privately with me.

From the offers made for Havanas and refused, the obtainable prices here to-day are certainly ¼ to ¾ franc higher than could have been had last week.

I remain, my dear Sir,

Yours very truly,

J. VANDERBILT.

ANTWERP, 13th *October*, 1865.

HY. THOMPSON, Esq.

DEAR SIR,—Having finished the examination of the damaged sugar per *John Howard*, I have made the following allowances instead of going to public sale, viz. :—

200 boxes badly damaged, 3s. per cwt.

419 ditto, more or less, 1s. 6d. „

Nine boxes are empty, and with some others half empty, I fear a heavy loss in weight, which, of course, underwriters have to allow for, as also the extra expenses caused by the damage.

The continued wet is retarding the unloading of the *American* and *Banker*, but I hope to be able to see part of the damaged sugar per *American* on Monday or Tuesday.

I am, Sir,

Your obedient Servant,

EDMUND PAGE.

ANTWERP, 19*th October*, 1865.

HY. THOMPSON, Esq.,
     London.

DEAR SIR,—Only to-day have I been able to inspect the sugar per *American*, the weather having been so wet. Of 393 boxes put aside, I found 158 sound; thus leaving 235 boxes damaged, upon which I have allowed 1*s.* per cwt. In this matter you save the expense which is usually incurred by the half-dozen certifying brokers.

To-morrow I shall inspect the sugar per *Banker* and *Ramoneur*. Thanking you for your favour of 18th inst.,

       I am, dear Sir,
         Your obedient Servant,
           EDMUND PAGE.

———

ANTWERP, 20*th October*, 1865.

HY. THOMPSON, Esq.,
     London.

DEAR SIR,—I beg to inform you that of the 287 boxes per *Banker*, put aside, I found 75 boxes sound, leaving 212 boxes damaged, upon which I have allowed 1*s.* per cwt.

Of the 131 per *Ramoneur*, put aside, I found 23 sound, leaving 108 damaged, upon which I have allowed 1*s.* 6*d.* per cwt., informing Messrs. Oke, Klenworth, and Co. thereof.

       I am, dear Sir,
         Your most obedient Servant,
           EDMUND PAGE.

(Order for Timber.)

LONDON.

GENTLEMEN,—I am in receipt of your favour quoting price for 800 loads of Dantzic oak, now lying in the Commercial Docks, which I accept, and you can draw on me for the amount named at three months, delivering one half of the timber at my wharf at your earliest convenience, and I will give you instructions shortly respecting the remainder.

I am, Gentlemen,
Your obedient Servant,
THOMAS DAY.

To Messrs. CHURCHILL & SIMS,
Timber Brokers.

(Offer of Tin.)

LONDON, *Jan.* 20, 1865.

GENTLEMEN,—We have just landed from Rotterdam some splendid blocks of tin of the finest quality, which we are able to sell at £92 per ton, payable at three months. Your order will be esteemed by

Your obedient Servants,
ULPH & Co.

To Messrs. C. ROCK & Co.

(Offer of Lead.)

SIR,—Some time ago you were inquiring our price for English pig lead, W. B. brand. We are now in a

position to sell some at £21 per ton, payable by bills at
two and three months.

We are, Sir,

Yours obediently,

SHERWOOD & Co.

To Messrs. C. ROCK & Co.

Quoting Prices of Iron.

LONDON, 20th July.

GENTLEMEN,—In answer to your favour of the 17th,
our price for supplying castings to the destination you
mentioned in your letter, is £4. 10s. per ton, of the best
pig-iron, carriage exclusive. Our terms are cash, one
month after delivery.

We remain, Gentlemen,

Yours obediently,

JACKSON & Co.

To Messrs. E. HOWITT & Co.

(Inquiry about Machinery.)

LONDON, May 26th, 1866.

SIR,—We will thank you to inform us your price and
terms for an engine and boiler, the former to lift about
three tons 200 feet high, in about one minute and a
half. Our building is located at the side of a canal,
and the object we seek is to receive and ship goods
with more convenience at our warehouses. We have
a building at one corner, in front, at present used as
a lumber-house. It occurs to us that this place will

suit for the engine and boiler-rooms. We may add that ample water can be had from the roof of our warehouse, there being a tank at that locality.

We are, Sir,
Yours obediently,
SHAND & Co.

To EDWIN WILMOT, Esq., C.E.

(Reply to foregoing.)

Offices—ADELPHI, May 28th, 1866.

GENTLEMEN,—I have the honour to acknowledge the receipt of your favour of the 26th inst. The price of the engine and boiler you require, exclusive of fixing, is £   (hundred pounds sterling). The terms are £   (hundred pounds) on signing the agreement, and the remainder, £   (hundred pounds) on the erection of the engine and boiler. The price for erecting will greatly depend on the present state of the site, &c.; but a fair estimate can be made by my surveying the locality, the charge for which will be ten guineas, including report.

I have the honour to be, Gentlemen,
Your obedient Servant,

To Messrs. SHAND & Co.   ED. WILMOT.

(Further Correspondence.)

June 8th, 1866.

SIR,—We are in receipt of your esteemed reply, dated the 28th ult. We agree to 'your price and terms

E 2

for the engine and boiler alluded to in our letter to you of the 26th ult., and will sign the agreement on the approval of our solicitor. We will thank you to survey the building intended to receive the engine and boiler at your earliest convenience, and on the receipt of your report we will proceed forthwith in the matter.

We remain,
Yours obediently,

To E. WILMOT, Esq., C.E.   SHAND & CO.

(Reply.)

Offices—ADELPHI, June 5th, 1866.

GENTLEMEN,—I beg to inform you that I yesterday surveyed the premises proposed as the site of your engine and boiler, and the conclusion I have arrived at is, that with a slight alteration the locality is suitable for the purpose. The enclosed agreement and report will render your solicitor and yourselves fully acquainted with the particulars as to price, terms, and time.

I am, Gentlemen,
Yours obediently,

To Messrs. SHAND & Co.   E. WILMOT.

(Advice of Dried Fruit Market.)

PATRAS, 27th September, 1865.

Messrs. JOSEPH TRAVERS & SONS,
      London.

DEAR SIRS,—We beg to confirm our respects of the 20th. Freights per steam to Liverpool having been reduced by rival companies to 20s. and 10 per cent., speculators have been encouraged to continue purchasing, notwithstanding the advices from your side, and the lowest price is 23 dollars, or 14s. 4d., free on board, excepting for perfect rubbish, which may be had in small lots, at 6d. less. Three steamers now loading for Liverpool will probably take nearly 5,000 tons.

London freights are 30s. to 35s. At Vostizza no price fixed yet.

We remain, &c.,

BARFF & Co.

(Letter of Introduction and Credit.)

LONDON, 5th April, 1866.

Messrs. BIGGAR, THOMSON, & Co.,
New York.

GENTLEMEN,—Mr. Belleyer, of the firm of Meyer Bros., Hamburg, is about to visit the principal cities of the United States, for the purpose of extending the business relations of his house in America. He sails either by the present or next mail steamer from Liverpool. Any information you can afford him, or introduction to houses in his line of business which you can give him, we shall duly esteem.

Although well supplied with funds, should he stand in need at any time of money, we will thank you to accommodate him on our account to the extent of £700 or £800, drawing upon us at a short date for your advances. Mr. Belleyer bears a letter of introduction from our house, and we append his signature at foot for your information.

Yours very truly,

HORROCKS & ROGERS.

Mr. Belleyer's signature,—*B. Belleyer.*

(Letter respecting Chemical Analyses.)

CHEMICAL LABORATORY,

March 27th, 1865.

DEAR SIR,—I have just received your letter, [which must have crossed one which I sent to you yesterday. I have heard nothing of the coals for analysis yet ; but if . Mr. Simmonds has ordered them to be forwarded to me, perhaps they will be delivered to-day or to-morrow.

I am sorry that you have been unsuccessful in getting the leaves of New Zealand flax from Dr. Hooker. Dry leaves would answer very well for the experiment, which I am very anxious to try, as the question is becoming more and more important daily.

Dear Sir, yours truly,

JOHN MERCER, Esq.   M. KEATES.

(Letter respecting Wool.)

BASINGHALL STREET,

20th January, 1865.

SIR,—In reply to your favour of yesterday's date, our market at this particular period is quite bare of any Colonial wools that would prove an acquisition to you. In a few weeks our new clip will be arriving, when we hope to have a good assortment of Port Phillip and Adelaide wools, but that from Sydney and Van Diemen's Land (good flocks) will be still later to arrive.

We shall be happy to oblige you with specimens, if you will give us your latest time for receiving them.

Yours respectfully,

HENRY P. HUGHES, Jun.

P. L. SIMMONDS, Esq.

(From a Foreign Correspondent.)

BOLOGNA, 20th April, 1865.

SIR,—Some time ago I received a letter from you, and I am sorry I have been unable to answer it sooner. I will send you a copy of the next number of my Journal, where you will see that your desire has been complied with. I beg you, in return, to mention the *Giornale d'Agricoltura* early in your *Technologist*. I also keep a store of agricultural implements ; if you think proper to send me some Whitney gins, or any other machinery, be pleased to write me the conditions. I, however, wish you would write in French or in Italian. In the mean time I send you the last number of my Journal, and I beg you to consider whether it might suit you to make a regular exchange of it with yours.

I wish I could visit the Dublin Exhibition, but I find I cannot ; I nevertheless thank you for your kind offers.

I am, Sir, yours sincerely,

Mr. P. L. SIMMONDS,   F. L. BOTTER.
London.

(Letter from the Customs.)

CUSTOM-HOUSE, LONDON,
22nd March, 1866.

SIR,—I am directed by the Commissioners of her Majesty's Customs to transmit to you herewith, in accordance with the request contained in your letter of the 14th inst., an account of the monthly receipt of packages from the several foreign countries represented in the Dublin International Exhibition, 1865, and an account showing the quantities of the foreign wines exhibited by the several wine-producing countries in the Dublin International Exhibition, which have been taken out for consumption in the United Kingdom.

I am, Sir,

Your most obedient Servant,

P. L. SIMMONDS, Esq.   GEO. DICKINS, *Secretary.*

(Approval of Machinery and Order for more.)

GENTLEMEN,—We have great pleasure in informing you that the machinery you made for our grinding department twelve months ago is in first-rate condition, and we cannot better express our satisfaction than by enclosing a cheque on account that you may commence another set exactly like the last, our trade having increased to that extent as to require new appliances.

We have the honour to be, Gentlemen,

Yours truly,   .

To Messrs. HUNT & Co.   P. DEVERUE & Co.

(Enclosure.)

(Reply to Foregoing.)

GENTLEMEN,—Your favour and the enclosed cheque duly came to hand, for which accept our thanks. We are pleased to hear that all the machinery is working well, and we shall always endeavour to sustain the reputation of our house for work turned out. Your esteemed order will be commenced to-morrow, and shall be completed and delivered forthwith.

We remain, Gentlemen, with thanks,
Yours obediently,
HUNT & Co.

To Messrs. DEVERUE & Co.

(To an Engineer, requiring his Attendance.)

SIR,—The machinery you erected for our mills some time back is daily getting more out of repair, and in fact so much so, that yesterday we incurred a delay of two hours. Your agreement with us, you may remember, requires that you will prevent all mishaps by your attendance as inspector. We take this opportunity of reminding you that you are under a penalty, which we shall be obliged to enforce if you do not immediately interest yourself in the matter.

We are, Sir,
Yours obediently,
A. YOUL & Co.

To R. NICHOL, Esq.

(Reply to an Order.)

August 7th, 1866.

Sir,—We shall have great pleasure in forwarding to you the goods you name in your favour of the 5th inst. As our terms are *cash* in advance, we will thank you to remit the same on the morning of the day you require the goods.

We are, Sir
Yours obediently,
Simons & Co.

Jacob Field, Esq.

(Letter of Introduction.)

London, *January 28th,* 1865.

My Dear Sir,—Mr. C. Pavia, a gentleman who has been connected with the superintendence branch of this office—the Italian Department—for the last nine months, and who was recommended by Mr. Heath, the Consul-General in London, to fill one of the responsible positions connected with the Exhibition, has requested me to give him a few lines to you to ask you whether you could perhaps interest yourself about him in connection with the "Permanent Exhibition" in London, of which you are a director?

Mr. Pavia will himself bring the certificate which Cavalier Devincenzi gave him, and which will speak for itself better than any recommendation, so that I will only add that if you could help him in any matter, you would be carrying out the wishes of Cavalier Devincenzi and myself; in this belief I beg to return you my best thanks beforehand, and am,

My dear Sir,

Yours truly

W. P. JERVIS

P. L. SIMMONDS, Esq.

(Letter of Introduction.)

30th August, 1865.

P. L. SIMMONDS, Esq.

DEAR SIR,—I beg leave to introduce to you my eldest son, a Government official of some twelve years' standing. He is now Landing Surveyor in the Customs Department; formerly chief clerk in the Audit-office. So, if you require statistical information, or particulars of the Colony generally, he will be able to give it.

He has been much out of health lately, and has twelve months' leave of absence to visit England. As he was a mere boy when he left his native land, he will feel almost a stranger when he arrives, and I shall esteem it a great favour if you will give him a little of your advice and direction in his desire to see a few sights in London. I know of no one so able as yourself, and I believe you will oblige me in this. He knows your friend Mr. Evans, and can give you a little information of him also.

With kind regards to all your family,

I am, Dear Sir,

Yours truly,

JOHN TAMBERLIK.

LETTERS TO FOREIGN CORRESPONDENTS.

——•✕•——

London, Sept. 5, 1865

Messrs. HENDERSON, BROTHERS, & Co.,

      Boston, U.S.

DEAR SIRS,—Enclosed I beg to hand you invoice of the first part of your order of the 7th Aug., and I hope to have the remainder, with the foreign goods, ready in a few days. B, L per next mail.

      Case mark, H. B. & Co.

        428.

I hope it will reach you in good condition.

I avail myself of the opportunity to ask you for a remittance for the balance of your account, £49. 10s. 7d., which I shall be pleased to receive as soon as convenient.

I am desirous of getting the latest Boston and New York Directories, and if you can obtain them for me, should be glad if they could be sent to me by an early mail.

      Yours truly,

        L. NICOLET.

————

London, 5th October, 1865.

Messrs. WILLIAMSON & DAVISON,

      Mauritius.

DEAR SIRS,—I am in receipt of your favours of the 10th Aug., and am glad to find you have disposed of my two consignments, per *Ellen Mary* and *Dione*, at a good price.

I am now preparing a further shipment, which I shall send in the course of this month, packed in tin as you recommend, and will wait on you by next mail with B/L and invoice. If any one article suits your market better than another, please advise me of it, that I may endeavour to conform to the requirements of the colony.

> I am, dear Sirs,
>> Yours very truly,
>>> HENRY WATSON.

(Remitting Money to meet Bills falling due.)

LONDON, 18*th June*, 1865.

Messrs. DALAS & Co.,
    Paris.

DEAR SIRS,—I received yours of the 14th inst., and herewith enclose Speilmann's draft for 3,500£. Please attend to the payment of the following drafts on you falling due at the dates named :—

		Fr.	
20th,	Croisy	445	50
24th,	Madok	2774	0
„	Mazzini............	212	44
„	Garibaldi	231	0
		Fr. 3662	94

> I am, dear Sirs,
>> Yours truly,
>>> EDWARD GILBERT.

LONDON, 16*th June*, 1865.

Mr. C. BARBOT, Tahiti.

DEAR SIR,—I have to acknowledge receipt of your letter of the 26th Feb., covering account sales for 1,254f. 50c. in my favour, and remitting me French Treasury Bill for 1,300f. I regret to find that business in your island continues so stagnant, but trust to have brighter accounts from you shortly. It is a great pity that there is no direct communication between your island and England and France, but that shipments have to be made to Sydney to wait opportunities of forwarding to Tahiti. The long-agitated steam route *viâ* Panama and Australia, touching at Tahiti, will, I hope, now soon be carried out, and thus give a stimulus to business in your island.

It is really deplorable to find that goods shipped to you from here in September, 1863, should only have come to hand in December, 1864. There are, I believe, two vessels despatched annually from Valparaiso to Tahiti. Would that mode of shipment be preferable, or transport by the way of San Francisco?

With respect to the error of which you complain in the quantity of combs sent by the *A. P. Sharp*, I have turned to the original order, and the word is clearly "gross," and not dozens. I will attend to the new instructions you give, to keep you more fully supplied with soaps, perfumes, and fashionable toilet articles.

I am, dear Sir,

Yours truly,

EDWARD ROBINSON.

(Transmitting Accounts for Collection.)

LONDON, *5th June*, 1865.

M. St. CASSEL, Madrid.

DEAR SIR,—I send you herewith a list of accounts due in your city and other towns for collection, some of which are of old date, and one or two drafts dishonoured, which require protest. I trust you will be able to recover of the gross amount about 12,000 reals, and remit it by the 27th to Mr. Leblanc, who has occasion for it for the payment of duties, &c.

Please make out your statement of account with me up to the end of the month, so that I may be able to balance my books for the half-year.

Yours truly,

J. A. CARRILL.

List of Accounts for Collection.

Morino Tersa,	Madrid............	2,680·47
Martin Luque,	„	1,179
Don Miro Cara,	„	351·50
Don Almagro Carol,	„	250
Don Limias, Jaen	....	1,027·10
Don Jose Sancho, Jerez	....	578·10
Don Espanol, Malaga	....	749·27
Don Carlos, Vieluna	....	1,117·60
Don Joachimo, Cadiz	....	2,782·10
Don Perez Herman, Lorca............		2,703·02

13,733·16

(Acknowledging Money and Advising Bill of Lading.)

LIVERPOOL.

Mr. WILSON, St. Lucia.

SIR,—Your favour of 31st March is to hand, with draft for £26 on the Colonial Bank, at 30 days' sight, which is placed to your credit with thanks. By next mail I shall, I hope, be able to send you invoices and B/L. I trust that the due and satisfactory execution of your commission will lead to further and more extensive orders.

Your obedient Servant,

S. FALCONER.

(Transmitting Invoices.)

LONDON.

Mr. C. ABRAHAM, Merchant,
           Kingston, Jamaica.

DEAR SIR,—Annexed I have the pleasure to hand you invoices of cases C. A. 1 to 4 per *Marquis of Argyll*, and C. A. 199/200, which have been shipped by your agent here, Mr. Isaacs. I hope these cases will reach you in good condition, and that the goods will give you satisfaction. I shall be very happy to find your orders increasing, and trust that for the future our transactions may be mutually profitable.

Awaiting the favour of your further commands,

I am,

Yours obediently,

PHILIP GLADSON.

(Enclosing Bills of Lading, &c.)

LONDON, *June*, 1865.

Messrs. WILKINS, COLLINS, & Co.,
 Melbourne.

DEAR SIRS,—I am in receipt of your favour of the 14th April, and regret to hear that your market continues depressed. Annexed please find duplicate invoices of the goods indented for, which I trust will be duly taken up, as agreed, on arrival. The B/L, per *Sea Star*, was sent you by last mail.

Your advices are so discouraging, that I have given up the idea of shipping any more to your market at present, considering that you have still on hand a large portion of my shipments, some of which date as far back as 1863. If, however, you can obtain indents for me on the same terms as the present, I shall be happy to execute them.

Yours very truly,
 JOHN HODGSON.

(Consenting to Consign and Advising Shipments.)

LONDON, *July*, 1865.

Messrs. ECCLES, BROWN, & Co.,
 Nelson, N. Z.

GENTLEMEN,—In conformity with the request of your London correspondents, we shall have much pleasure in making you quarterly consignments of books and stationery, commencing with the present invoice of seven cases despatched per *Caduceus*, which sailed from London on the 13th June. We hope these cases will reach you in good condition, realize profitable prices, and lead to a continuance of business.

B/L enclosed, awaiting receipt of your advices.

> We are, Gentlemen,
> Your obedient Servants,
> KENDRICK & JONES.

(Advising Shipment of Perfumery.)

LONDON, 16*th July*, 1866.

Messrs. JONES & Co., Boston, U.S.

DEAR SIRS,—I beg to enclose duplicate invoices of your kind orders—the London part per *Columbia*, of which B/L in my next; and the Paris part per *Adriatic* steamer, for which you will receive B/L in due course from Messrs. Prescott & Son. The remaining part of your Paris order will shortly follow per sailing vessel as ordered. I have taken the liberty of adding to the latter $\frac{1}{4}$ of a gross of Prince of Wales Bouquet, as per enclosed label, as I think it likely there will be a run for that article on account of the forthcoming visit of the Prince of Wales to the States. Shall be happy to send you more if you approve of it. The price of bouquets got up in that style will be 25*s*. per gross. I can send you any perfumes, with the same sort of label, which I think would take well, being a novelty. It is the style I have adopted for my Paris depôt, and the label is much admired. As many Americans buy these extracts retail there, I think it would be policy to send the same to you in future.

I have made arrangements with Mr. Morris to select some first-rate retail store in New York, to be named in their advertisements of my perfumery, so that the public may know where to get them. I think it would be as well to do the same for Boston, and if you can get any retailer there to take up my goods with spirit, his name shall be inserted in the Boston advertisements. In that case please send his name to Mr. Morris, and he will have it inserted, as I leave him the charge of attending to all my advertisements in America. The names of my wholesale agents will only be inserted in the American Druggists' Circular.

I remain, dear Sirs,

Yours truly,

J. W. WILSON.

(Letter of Thanks with Advice of Shipment.)

Mr. R. MATHESON, Caraccas.

DEAR SIR,—Your letter of the 23rd April is to hand, and I am very thankful to you for your kind information respecting the commercial productions of your State.

Enclosed I beg to hand you statement of account, and shall feel obliged by a remittance with further order.

Yours truly,

RICHARD THOMSON.

1865.

Jan.	1.	Balance	£103	3	0
March	17.	To goods, nett	12	10	3
„	30.	Charges per *Midlothian* ...	1	2	6
April	4.	To goods, nett	39	18	5

£156 14 2

Feb. 20. Cr. Bank draft 50 0 0

£106 4 2

(Order for Gold Thread.)

MADRAS, *June 5.*

Messrs. JOHNSON, SIMONS, & Co.

GENTLEMEN,—I am open to take 1,000 ounces more of your fine gold, dark-coloured thread, at 7s. ; the cost, as in the last instance, to be paid by me in four months after receipt of the thread. If not good and of uniform colour, the thread will be sold at your risk. If you agree to these terms, you can ship the thread at your convenience.

W. H. SMITH.

(Letter of Advice of Consignment.)

LONDON, *26th June.*

Messrs. LEVY & MOORE,
    New York.

DEAR SIRS,—Annexed we beg to send you invoices (the account of charges being separate) for cases L. & M. 229/30, which we hope will reach you in good condition. This small trial we believe, may induce you to open larger transactions with us, which will be profitable to both parties, especially if you keep up the regular price of our goods in the States. B/L have been forwarded by the shipping agent.

About the beginning of next month we shall send you the second part of your kind order.

Hoping your Mr. Levy has had a pleasant voyage back and has returned safe,

We remain, dear Sirs, yours very truly,

A. WRIGHT & Co.

(Reply to Claim for Deficiencies.)

LONDON, *July 1st*, 1866.

Messrs. CHANDLER & Co.,
    Rouen.

GENTLEMEN,—I have the details of your claim for short receipts in cases E & H 1, and A 9. I am quite ready to allow you what I consider just and fair, viz.,

53—1 doz. @ 24f. less 15 per cent.......	Fr. 20 40
Carriage ditto...................	9 00
	Fr. 29 40

or £1. 3s. 10d.

The other things being short only, I believe, through the defaults of the Customs and Octroi officers, I do not consider I am liable for them.

I hope this will prove satisfactory, and on receipt of your answer I will send you a credit note for the amount.

Yours truly,

MORGAN LEE.

(Reply to Foreign House as to Discount, &c.)

LONDON, *August*, 1866.

Messrs. SANGER & Co.,

Pernambuco.

DEAR SIRS,—Your favour is duly to hand. I cannot account for your not having received my May letter, except that it may have been posted late for the mail. As regards your complaint of my supplying other people in your town, the extent of my promise to you was that I would not execute any direct orders for your district, and to that I have kept; but it is quite impossible for me to refuse orders given me by merchants or commission agents who do not state for what market they buy, and feel offended if I ask them. You will not find any house in the trade that would accept such an unreasonable engagement. My invariable terms are these : 10 per cent. discount £50, and 15 per cent. above, for cash on delivery. You get, therefore, six months' credit, and 5 per cent. more than most. Coupling this with the commission the buyers on your side have to pay to their agents, I think it leaves you a fair margin for profit.

With all the desire I have of keeping up and extending our connection, I cannot possibly increase your discount with the present term of six months (which is sometimes extended to twelve). But as you seem to say that credit is of no advantage to you, I am ready to exchange it for an extra 5 per cent., that is to say, I will allow you 20 per cent. instead of 15 per cent., if you send me cash with the orders. This will give you a clear 5 or 10 per cent. advantage over others. As regards present orders in hand, I think it better not to delay them until your reply, and, to prevent disappointment, send them on the old terms.

> I remain, dear Sir,
> > Yours truly,
> > > S. SAMUDAR.

(Agreeing to consign, and suggesting terms.)

SHEFFIELD, 19th June.

Messrs. BONNEY & Co.,
Nelson, N. Z.

GENTLEMEN,—I am in receipt of your letter of the 31st March, and acting upon the high recommendation of Messrs. Sydney & Co., and the promise you hold out of occupying yourself energetically in the placing and sale of my goods in your colony, I beg to entrust to your care a case of goods ordered by a firm in your town; and of which the invoice is enclosed. Please deliver it on payment of freight and charges, &c. By the next ship I shall send you a first consignment on sale, but as I am not quite sure what are the most suitable articles for your market, either in cutlery, plated goods, or hardware, I forward by this mail one of our price currents for you to select from. I doubt not a considerable business may be done in the different provinces of New Zealand, but the delay in return proceeds causes me to be scrupulous in extending consignments. I accept the terms you propose for doing business, but I would observe that the best means of increasing confidence and extending business will be prompt remittances. I fancy that consignments every three months will be quite sufficient to meet your requirements, and half-yearly account-sales and returns will, I trust, render our business relations mutually agreeable and remunerative.

Believe me to be, Gentlemen,
Your very obedient Servant,
F. WARDER.

(Acknowledging Money and Execution of Order.)
LONDON, July.

J. NESSERWANGER, Esq.,
    Kurrachee.

SIR,—We are in receipt of your favour of 4th May, containing your draft for £5.   Annexed we have the pleasure to send you invoice of your kind order, which has been sent as requested through Messrs. Smith, Elder, & Co., and which we hope will meet with your approval.

Yours truly,
ROBINSON & BELLEVILLE.

(Acknowledging Remittance.)
LONDON, 29th June, 1865.

Messrs. KOSSMAN & Co., Sydney.

DEAR SIRS,—I have the pleasure of acknowledging the receipt of your draft at 60 days, Commercial Banking Company of Sydney, value £100, for which amount you are duly credited, with best thanks.

I hope the next mail will bring me a good order from you, as I have to regret being a very long time deprived of your favours.

Waiting your further commands,
I remain, dear Sirs,
Yours truly,
EDWD. GIBES.

(Advising Acceptance of Draft, and urging prompt execution of Order.)

LIVERPOOL, *May 24, 1866.*

Messrs. J. VOGELSANG & SOHN,
　　Hayda, in Bohemia.

DEAR SIRS,—Your favour of the 10th instant is to hand. Enclosed I return, accepted, your draft for £24. 7s., for which amount please give me credit.

I am in great want of the two gross of cut bottles ordered, and shall feel much obliged by your sending them forward without delay.

Your obedient Servant,
　　　　A. DUMARGEST.

(Acknowledging Account and forwarding Money.)

Messrs. HEROT & DANVER,
　　Paris.

GENTLEMEN,—I am in receipt of yours of the 22nd instant, forwarding your account current, which, on examination, I find correct.　Enclosed you have a letter of credit at sight on Spielmann & Co. of your city, for 12,500 francs, with which please credit me, and apply proceeds as follows in liquidation of drafts falling due.

27th	Fr. 1,705 25	Perouse.
30th	5,000 0	Farquhar.
	2,841 25	Yapp.
	1,000 0	Berthollet.

Fr. 10,546 50

Believe me. Gentlemen, to be,
　　Your obedient Servant,
　　　　MARTIN PIGNEAU.

Messrs. IVENS & Co., New York.

DEAR SIRS,—Your favour of the 3rd inst. arrived while I was away from home ; hence the reason it was not replied to sooner. I send you now duplicate invoices of my shipments, and shall take care in future to send you separate invoices for each ship. The discount of 10 per cent. is an error, as you presumed ; the prices are nett, which has been rectified in the enclosed.

As regards your complaint of my sending goods by steamer instead of sailing vessel, I believe your Mr. Jones's instructions were to send the extracts in tin by steamers and other goods by sailing vessels, which has been done. I do not see that anything has been sent by *Adriatic.* They were shipped as follows :—

Case 223, Extracts in tin, per *Europa* str. freight $5 50
  „   245,   „   „   *Arabia*   „   6 14
  „   254, 55, Merchandise, *Sanscrit*, sailg. vessel   2 0
  „   103—110,   „   *Columbia*,   „   £2 4 8

So that, after all, the freight amounts to little, considering the value of the goods. As to the choice of the steamers, I beg to observe that I leave that to your agent, Mr. Turnbull.

Yours truly,

Two enclosures.   JOHN JONES.

July 31st, 1866.

Mr. ROSE, Hamburg.

DEAR SIR,—Herewith I forward statement of account to date, with draft on you for £16. 9s. 5d., to balance same, which please kindly accept and return.

Yours truly,

Two enclosures.   JAMES FERGUSON.

STATEMENT OF ACCOUNT FOR YEAR 1866.

Dr.]		£	s.	d.			Cr.]	£	s.	d.
Jan. 1.	Balance	30	19	7	Feb. 29.	Draft		16	14	0
" 12.	Goods, nett	13	14	0	Mar. 20.	Cash		24	12	8
Feb. 16.	" "	10	4	3	" "	" from Jones		3	0	0
Jan. 27.	" Paris	12	18	5	" "	Advertisements		3	6	10
Feb. 15.	" "	9	5	8	June 5.	Bill 10 Sept.		50	0	0
" 24.	" "	4	16	8	" "	" 29 "		50	0	0
Mar. 22.	" "	82	5	2	" 19.	Cash, Jones		9	3	4
Apl. 12.	" "	13	7	6		Error		0	16	2
" 26.	" "	10	13	3		Draft		27	11	4
June 9.	" "	12	7	0	" "	Advertisements		2	11	4
" 8.	" "	9	8	6	Discount omitted Feb. 15			1	16	2
" 26.	" "	6	7	6	" " 24			0	0	8
" 27.	" "	13	15	8	" March 22			16	9	0
					" April 26			2	2	2
					Balance			29	19	2
		£238	2	8				£233	2	3
	Balance	29	19	2	July 6.	Draft		22	4	2
July 1.	Goods	8	11	0	" 31.	"		16	9	5
" 31.	" "	0	3	5						
		£38	13	7				£38	13	7

(Forwarding Statement of Account, and advising Draft for Balance.)

LONDON, *Dec.* 10*th*, 1864.

Messrs. GOODHART & Co., Hong Kong.

GENTLEMEN,—With this you have statement of account to date, showing balance to date of £376. 3*s.*, for which we shall draw on you at thirty days through the Oriental Bank, by next mail.

Yours truly,

DEARN, BRABY, & Co.

———

Messrs. GOODHART & Co., Hong Kong, *in account with* DEARN, BRABY, & Co.

1858.		£.	s.	d.
May 20. Goods per *Taffity*		30	3	7
„　　„　　„ *Menislaus*		185	14	10
June 10. „　　„ *Versailles*		32	1	1
July 27. „　　„ *Menai*		9	11	1
„　„　　„　„ *Hero of Alma*		7	14	10
„　3. „ from Paris		80	14	10
„ 23. „　　„　　„		13	3	3
„ 22. Consignment from Paris		23	11	0
„　　　„　　„ London ...		27	17	0
Freight, &c. „　　„　...		3	9	0
		£414	0	6
Cr. Draft, 15th Oct., 1858......		60	0	0
		£354	0	6
5 per cent. on £354, 15 months		22	2	6
Net Balance............		£376	3	0

(Acknowledging Account Sales.)

LONDON, *10th August*, 1866.

Messrs. HALLETT & Co.,
    Adelaide.

DEAR SIRS,—I am in receipt of your favour of the 12th June, enclosing account sales of my shipments per *Cissy*, and draft for same, £24. 3s. 4d., which is satisfactory, and for which I return you my best thanks. I will prepare another miscellaneous shipment, and send on towards the end of this month, trusting it will meet with a good market on arrival. I enclose B/L of my shipment per *Windward*, of which I sent you invoice per last mail.

        I remain,
           Yours truly,
              S. MARSHALL.

(Instructions to close Consignment.)

HULL, *June*, 1864.

Messrs. EBELTHORPE & Co., Shanghai.

DEAR SIRS,—Deprived of your favours for a very long time, the object of the present is to bring to your recollection my consignment to your house, per *Mermaid*, in May, 1863, which I am afraid has escaped your notice, and to request, if all is not yet sold, that you will send the remainder immediately to auction, to close this long-standing matter.

I suppose your business is of too important a nature to allow you to pay much attention to stationery, which accounts for the delay in disposing of this parcel, for some consignments I have sent since to another house have always sold immediately at good prices, and some were " to arrive."

> I remain, dear Sirs,
> Yours truly,
> ALGERNON WHITE.

(Reply to Correspondent in India as to Sales and Consignments.)

> LONDON, 10th *August*, 1866.

S. SIMLINSON, Esq., Calcutta.

DEAR SIR,—I am in receipt of your favour of 22nd June, enclosing account sales of my consignment per *Mersey*, showing £42 to your debit. I am much obliged for your consideration in not charging commission, and accept of it this time, the loss being heavy on cost. If such heavy duties are charged on soaps, I must leave off shipping them except to order, as they would not pay at all. I think it is somewhat arbitrary of the Customs to fix a value on soap so much higher than can be realized for it, but I suppose we have nothing to do but to submit.

The account I sent you on 26th May would, I presume, reach you shortly after despatch of your last. I therefore do not send you a fresh one, as you can make it up yourself by adding account sales as realized by you, and deducting your remittances.

Annexed I send you invoice of a first shipment per *Empress*, with B/L of same and reduced invoices, although I suppose the latter is not of much use, from what you write me.

I regret you have been unable to obtain me the

sandal-wood oil, but I would not advise you to give more than 12 annas per oz. for it, as I can get the very best kind in Paris for 70£ per kilog., equal to 1s. 8d. per oz., and generally the Indian is less in favour there than that drawn in this country.

I shall await account sales per *William and James* to repeat my shipments of Paris goods, as there may be some articles which sell better than others, and it will serve me as a guide.

I am sorry to say I have no further news to report of the garnets, the market for them being perfectly stagnant. I was in hopes of going to Neufchatel myself respecting them, but have been prevented hitherto by pressure of business. I have, however, placed some samples in the hands of a friend at Bale, who promises to endeavour to effect a sale. I would not advise you to buy any more until part of the last shipment, if not all, has moved off.

Yours truly,

R. FOSTER.

(The same.)

LONDON, *August 28th*, 1866.

S. SIMLINSON, Esq., Calcutta.

DEAR SIR,—I am in receipt of your kind favour dated 7th July, with account sales per *William and James,* which are very satisfactory; also the £100 bank-draft, with which you are credited, with best thanks. I am also greatly obliged for the advantage in the exchange.

I have nothing fresh to report respecting the garnets

alluded to in my last, and would advise you to buy no more at any price, as they are a perfect drug in the market. I am afraid it will be impossible to find a purchaser for a long while ; my correspondent in Germany has been unable to find sale for them in Bohemia.

I remain, dear Sir,

Yours truly,

R. FOSTER.

(Order to Purchase Produce on certain limits.)

LONDON, *May*, 1866.

Messrs. DUNCAN & BURNS,

Bahia.

DEAR SIRS,—I shall be glad if you can purchase for me 3,000 to 4,000 double bundles of Piassava fibre : if deliverable f. o. b. at £7. 10*s.* per ton (probably you may be able to get them shipped as dunnage); 8 to 10 tons of dry and salted hides @ 4*d.* per lb. ; 50 or 60 logs of rosewood, at 700 reis the arroba, and 20 barrels of tapioca, at the lowest current rates. Both the latter articles seem to be declining in price in your market. Please ship such of these as are to be obtained at my limit by first ship to Liverpool, sending me bills of lading and particulars for insurance by mail steamer.

Yours truly,

JOHN MORGAN.

APPLICATIONS FOR MONEY & REPLIES, &c.

———•◦•———

(Application for Money.)

29th May, 1866.

SIR,—Our Collector will have the pleasure of calling upon you on Friday morning next for settlement of our account.

Thanking you for your kind favours, which shall at all times command our prompt attention,

We remain,
Yours respectfully,
MALCOLMSON & Co.

Amount of Account, £5. 7s. 6d.

P.S.—If absent from home, please leave instructions to pay our Collector, as it is a long way to call for so small an amount.

———————

(Notifying inability to meet acceptances, and asking renewal.)

GENTLEMEN,—We regret to inform you that our acceptances drawn by you, payable on the   inst., cannot be met, owing to the failure of the firm of Messrs. Alder and Co., of Liverpool.

In order to preserve confidence with our customers and

G

yourselves, we solicit a renewal, at   per cent., payable
three months after date.

Trusting this arrangement will meet with your approval,

We are, Gentlemen,

Yours obediently,

NASH & Co.

To Messrs. MANSFIELD & Co.

LONDON.

GENTLEMEN,—Your advice of the   inst. duly came
to hand.   We thank you for drawing on us for the sum
of £500, payable in Berlin, 60 days after sight.   Such
an arrangement will ensure our meeting present and
future liabilities with certainty.   We enclose the draught
accepted, dated the 15th inst., and will be most happy to
continue our purchases of you forthwith.

We are, Gentlemen,

Yours obediently,

ROBERT AMOS & SONS.

To Messrs. C. FARLOW & Co.

SIR,—Kindly accept the enclosed bill for £55, payable
at three months after date.   We are much in want of
ready money, or we would not thus press you.   Your
further orders will be esteemed by

Yours obediently,

HARRIS & Co.

To JOHN MACGREGOR, Esq.

GENTLEMEN,—I was greatly surprised on presenting your bill for £57, at Messrs. Glyn & Co.'s, yesterday, that it was returned. As, however, I do not wish to be the means of putting you to further expense than noting, &c., let me know *immediately* if you can arrange the matter before 2.30 this day.

I am, Sir,

Yours obediently,

MARTIN SEDLEY.

Messrs. THOMPSON & Co.,
   Whitefriars.

LIVERPOOL, May, 1866.

SIR,—We shall feel greatly obliged if you will remit us a cheque for the goods supplied you in December last. Our accounts are balanced every twelve months, and your default prevents us from closing our books for the date alluded to.

We are, Sir,

Yours obediently,

R. NICHOL & Co.

To JAMES HOLT, Esq.

LONDON, July, 1866.

Messrs. RAINSFORTH & THOMAS.

GENTLEMEN,—In reply to your note of this day, I beg to inform you that I accept the composition of 6s. in the £ offered by Boutellier.

The amount due to me is correct—£22. 8s. 5d.

GILBERT WILSON.

G 2

Messrs. WETHERBY & Co., City.

GENTLEMEN,—I am in receipt of your draft for
£16. 10s. 5d., which is duly placed to credit of your account.   As regards the concluding remark in your letter,
I beg to state that my terms are cash on receipt of invoice.
You will please note this in future.

Your obedient Servant,
ALEX. MASTERMAN.

Messrs. HOPCROFT, Poole.

DEAR SIRS,—Enclosed I beg to hand you cheque for
the amount of your account, £30. 11s. 6d.   Please acknowledge, and return statement receipted.

I am, dear Sirs,
Yours truly,
J. LADD.

OLD BROAD STREET, LONDON,
June 16th, 1866.

Messrs. PALMER & HOLT,
      Manchester.

GENTLEMEN,—Enclosed I beg to hand you bill for ac
ceptance, £216. 14s. 6d., which I shall feel obliged by
your returning me in course of post with the needful.

I am, Gentlemen,
Your obedient Servant,
WATT BURROUGHS.

SIR,—I beg to draw your attention to the enclosed account, which is long overdue, and beg to state that if it is not settled forthwith, I shall be compelled to place it for collection in the hands of the Society for the Protection of Traders.

J. ARROWSMITH.

Mr. HOOKER, Oxford.

SIR,—As your account was not settled with Mr. Carstairs when in Oxford, and is considerably overdue, I must request remittance of the balance per return of post. Amount £19. 2s.

I am, Sir,
Your obedient Servant,
FREDK. BATSON.

June 14, 1865.

Mr. RAIKES, Liverpool.

SIR,—As I have received no reply to my two letters requesting remittance for amount of your bill returned unpaid, I beg to say that unless I receive the amount by Saturday morning next, I shall place the matter in my solicitor's hands.

I am, Sir,
Your obedient Servant,
R. MOUAT.

(Consenting to hold over a Bill.)

LONDON, *Aug.* 1866.

SIR,—I have to acknowledge receipt of your application for extension of time to meet your acceptance, and although your payments have been somewhat irregular for some time, yet I will accommodate you once more by holding over your bill till this day week, when I trust to your punctual remittance to meet it.

Your obedient Servant,

T. ADDISON.

(To a Traveller on the Continent.)

DEAR SIR,—Your kind favour of the 18th is to hand. I do not wish to be harsh with Bernard, but you can press him, and hint at legal proceedings, so as to get some money out of him. I am glad to hear that you are about to send forward several good orders; the greatest care shall be given to their execution, and I hope they will lead to some important transactions for your next journey. I think Jenkins has only the commission on orders taken by himself. Of course I should not like to see you lose by it; therefore, as you say, we will discuss this matter on your return. Let me know by first post if you are going again to Prague, or further on.

If possible, I should like to send you the samples you require, for which please give me the names and quantities; and I shall also be glad to know if you can collect some outstanding accounts due at Vienna. Awaiting your prompt reply,

I am, yours truly,

THOS. FOGG.

(Complaint of Non-payment of Acceptance.)

Mr. CRAWLEY, Hastings.

SIR,—I am in receipt of your favour with £25, on account of the bill dishonoured. I am rather surprised at your not meeting this bill, as it has already been renewed once, and it puts me to considerable inconvenience, as the bill was paid into my bankers' before I received your letter, and I had great difficulty in preventing its being noted.

I shall feel obliged by your obviating this in future, by meeting your acceptances with promptitude.

I am, Sir,

Your obedient Servant,

S. SLATER.

(Acknowledging Dividend, and complaining of conduct of customer.)

H. STONNER, Esq., Cirencester.

SIR,—I beg to acknowledge receipt of your favour enclosing £6. 16s. 10d. dividend on Mr. Hope's estate, which is duly passed to credit. As regards your request to allow Mr. Hope to continue business without superintendence, I may state that when I allowed him time, it was with the understanding that he would continue purchasing goods from me, paying cash for the same. Now I find by my books that all he has paid for the last two years has been £1. 5s. Under these circumstances, I do not feel inclined to show him the same leniency that I would otherwise have done.

Your obedient Servant,

JAMES LUCY.

(Acknowledging Settlement of Account, and pointing out an Error.)

Messrs. HALLET & Co.,
        Tewkesbury.

DEAR SIR,—I was favoured on Saturday with a visit from Mr. Smith, who settled your account by accepting a bill at one month, from 24th July, for £88. 13s. 3d., payable at Glyn & Co.'s. On making up, however, the statement again, marking the destination of each parcel, as desired by Mr. S., I found that you had not been allowed discount on the invoice 31st May, in the statement previously delivered. This makes a difference of £2. 18s. 3d. standing to your credit on next transaction. I would have returned you the bill, but that it is already discounted.

                I remain, dear Sir,
                        Yours truly,
                                JACOB THOMPSON.

(Complaining of long credit taken.)

Mr. ROBINSON, Pembroke.

DEAR SIR,—On looking over my books, I observe that you have been in the habit for some time past of settling your account at twelve months instead of six months, as is done by my other customers. I have no objection to continue granting you that credit if you require it, but in that case, I think it right to inform you that you will not be entitled to discount on future payments, as I can only allow it on current six months' accounts. Should

you wish to save your discount, you will please remit me
the balance of the account last delivered to you.

> I remain, dear Sir,
> Yours truly,
> R. DAVENPORT.

(Complaining of a renewed bill not being met.)

LONDON, 27th *July*, 1866.

Mr. CONNOLLY,
> Northampton.

SIR,—I am really much surprised at the way you
treat me. After renewing your bill to oblige you, you then
fail to meet it, and only send me £20 on account; thus
giving me the trouble of writing half a dozen letters for
the paltry balance of £8. 13s. If the amount were
large, I might assume that you could not send it; but as
it is so small, I can only think that you will not do it,
and I must say it is a very uncourteous return for the
accommodation I have always been ready to give you. I
trust this is the last time I shall have to write for it.

> Yours obediently,
> PHILIP JONES.

(Asking permission to draw for amount due.)

10th *August*, 1866.

Mr. PETERLAND.

DEAR SIR,—Will you allow me to draw upon you at
three months for the goods supplied to you in May last,
£41. 15s. 3d., which were sold on six months' credit.

I shall also be happy to receive your further commands.

> Yours truly,
> JOHN ROBINSON.

———————

To the MANAGER of the UNION BANK,
　　Chancery Lane.

DEAR SIR,—Please discount the following bills and place to the credit of my account :—

$$\begin{array}{rrr} \pounds. & s. & d. \\ 44 & 10 & 7 \\ 88 & 13 & 3 \\ 193 & 6 & 5 \end{array} \right\} \pounds326 \ 10 \ 3$$

> With thanks,
> Yours truly,
> HY. DENNY.

LETTERS RESPECTING SHIPMENTS, &c.

(From Pickford & Co., respecting Shipment of Cases.)

CASTLE, WOOD STREET,
LONDON, E.C., *26th May*, 1866.

M. 826.

P. L. SIMMONDS, Esq.,
8, Winchester Street,
Pimlico, S.W.

SIR,—Referring to our M. 370 24th ult., we beg to remind you that the two cases consigned to Com. Strickland, Malta, care of Captain Bawden, H.M.S. "Supply," Woolwich, are still on hand; they remain entirely at the owner's risk and expense, and we shall be glad to receive early instructions for their disposal.

We are, Sir,
Your obedient Servants,
PICKFORD & Co.,
Per C. LUTTERTHWAITE.

(From Shipping Agent.)

46, LEADENHALL STREET, LONDON,
3rd April, 1865.

P. L. SIMMONDS, Esq.

DEAR SIR,—The "Eastern Province" is here in the Victoria Docks. I have entered the packages from

Natal for you, and have put them in the hands of our lighterman, who will bring them up, and ship them per Dublin boat as quickly as possible. They are as follows :—

$$
\begin{array}{l}
\left.\begin{array}{l} - \ 1 \\ \text{A} \ 1 \\ \text{B} \ 1 \end{array}\right\} \text{Cases} \\
\quad \text{C} \ 1 \ \text{Package} \\
\left.\begin{array}{l} \text{D} \ 1 \\ \text{E} \ 1 \end{array}\right\} \text{Cases}
\end{array}\right\} \text{ and 5 pairs of Horns.}
$$

Your printed labels will be attached.

Yours truly,

WM. HADEN.

(From Shipping Agent advising Shipment of Goods.)

46, LEADENHALL STREET, LONDON,

10th April, 1865.

P. L. SIMMONDS, Esq.

DEAR SIR,—Your favour and parcel of the 4th duly received.

You ought to have some of the packages by this time. In case your name should not be upon the cases from E. R. Power, Esq., you will find they are marked with his initials, E. R. P. I know they were at the wharf last week. The case of Malachite I saw put into the barge myself; your name was *painted* upon that package. Sometimes the paper addresses get torn, or rubbed off.

I enclose mate's receipt for the Natal goods per Dublin boat. She sailed this morning. Messrs. Hewitt sent off 22 packages by the Dublin boat of Saturday. I gave them the usual shipping note ; they are all labelled " To the Executive Committee." I gave them one of the bills, to get others printed of a similar character. They will have 8 or 10 more packages, I hope, by the boat of next Saturday.

The Union Company's mail steamer due at Southampton 15th to 18th inst., discharges *all* her cargo there.

I told Mr. Hill, the agent, to write you for instructions; it will save expense if they are put on board the Irish boat at Southampton.

I shall be glad to hear how you get on, and please send me a list of all the goods that have come to hand, that I may satisfy the senders.

Yours most obediently,
WM. HADEN.

(Reply to Application respecting Goods Exported)

SOUTHAMPTON, *6th April*, 1865.

P. L. SIMMONDS, Esq.

SIR,—I am in receipt of your favour of the 4th inst., and will give my best attention to your instructions respecting the packages expected from Natal by the next mail steamer, which is due here about the 17th.

Your obedient Servant,
WM. T. HILL,
Per GEO. THOMPSON.

(Letter respecting the Shipment of Salmon Ova to Australia.)

WARATAH HOUSE, CLAPHAM PARK, LONDON,
Jan. 26*th*, 1866.

SIR,—I beg leave to enclose you bill of lading for 141
boxes of salmon, salmon-trout, and brown trout ova, all
packed in an ice-house in the ship *Lincolnshire*, and consigned to you on behalf of the Salmon Commissioners of
Tasmania and the Acclimatization Society of Victoria.
These boxes contain about 87,000 salmon ova, 15,000 sea
or white trout ova, 500 brown trout ova ; total, 102,500 ;
and more particularly described as to marks in an enclosed
memorandum.

One hundred and two boxes, containing about 70,000
eggs, were stowed away in the best possible condition in
the best place, viz., at the bottom of the ice-house. I had
room for at least 30,000 more beside these, and waited
until the very last moment in the hope of getting that
number, when I was compelled to fill up the space with
ice, to my great grief, because I am of opinion that
10,000 there would arrive at Melbourne with more living
ova than 30,000 in any other place in the glaciarium. I
may be mistaken, and perhaps the top of the ice where I
was forced to put them will prove equally good with the
bottom.

I have also placed in the ice-house a box containing
cocoons of the Ailanthus silkworm, a present from the
Acclimatization Society of Paris ; and also, as an experiment, half a dozen fresh-laid hens' eggs, to see if they
will hatch in Melbourne.

Six choice apple-trees, two boxes choice bulbs, and last, but not least, two bundles containing varieties of Scotch heather, hoping grouse may soon be added to salmon, and when they arrive they may have the luxury of feeding on their native heather.

I had made preparations to have sent at least 150,000 ova, and four days of fine weather in the first or second weeks of January would easily have enabled the persons I had employed to obtain the required number, and without one shilling more expense.

We never had so much time before to get our ova; but the continued wet weather—rain, rain—so swelled the rivers, that the fishermen could not use their nets, neither could the fish be seen on their spawning-beds, the water was so thick and muddy. It required all the encouragements I could give to induce the several parties to continue what they wrote to me repeatedly was a hopeless task; but I was confident of success, and instructed them to offer one, or two, or even five pounds to the first fisherman who caught a spawning fish.

The following persons were engaged to get the ova, and they all contributed to the *Norfolk's* shipment; viz.— Mr. Ramsbottom, sen., of Clitheroe; his son, Mr. Westall Ramsbottom; Mr. F. Allies, of Worcester, and Mr. Thomas Johnson. They were directed to fish in the different rivers in the order of their names—the Ribble and Hodden, near Clitheroe; the Itchen and its tributaries, near Southampton; the Severn and Teme, near Worcester; and the Tyne and Tweed.

It is worth remarking that those who were most successful before were the least so this time, but not from

any fault or want of exertion on their part.   The following is the result of the two shipments :—

	Norfolk, 1864.	Lincolnshire, 1866.
Ramsbottom, sen.	18,000	41,000
Ramsbottom, jun.	50,000	16,000
Allies	40,000	500
Johnson	10,000	45,000
Totals	118,000	102,500

I have much pleasure in stating that the ice-house is
better constructed than any before, owing to having more
time.   The ice is, if anything, a little better ; so is the
moss, and the ova, and I trust the experiment will prove
as successful as the *Norfolk's.*

I am, Sir,
Your obedient Servant,
JAMES A. YOUL.

Mr. G. SPRIGG, Secretary,
Acclimatization Society, Melbourne.

———

(From the same.)

WARATAH HOUSE, CLAPHAM PARK, LONDON,
Jan. 26th, 1866.

SIR,—I beg leave respectfully to bring under the
notice of the Council of your Society the meritorious
conduct of Mr. Thomas Johnson, who, the moment he
had completed the ice-house on board of the *Lincolnshire,*
at my request started off to the Tweed to collect ova,
and succeeded, after the most untiring exertions, in

sending me 45,000. Unfortunately he met with a most serious accident, by slipping from a stone in the frost; but, notwithstanding he was not able to put his foot to the ground, he contrived to direct the operation of the fishermen, and persuaded his elder brother, living at Newcastle, to make two journeys up to London with two lots of ova.

I am quite certain that even a piece of parchment, framed, containing the Council's acknowledgment of his services in the cause of acclimatization, would be highly esteemed by him ; and I should consider any acknowledgment of the kind as a personal favour to a most deserving young man, who has aided me more than any other person in the three experiments I have made, and in the most disinterested manner.

I enclose for perusal three letters received from him after his accident, which prove his zeal and thoughtfulness. These I will feel obliged by your forwarding to the Hon. R. Officer, when the Council have done with them.

There were thirty tons of ice put into the house ; but from the very mild, warm weather whilst packing, it did not get frozen into one solid mass, like the *Norfolk's*, when we had from 13 to 20 degrees of frost. It is therefore possible more will melt on the voyage.

I cannot tell you by this mail the cost. It will be over £600, but I think under £700.

I have drawn £400 for account of the Government of Tasmania, and £200 on your Society's account. Full particulars next mail.

I have insured the ova for £700.

The *Lincolnshire* was run into whilst at anchor off

Gravesend by a brig, and had to return to dock to be repaired. I hope the ova will not be injured by the concussion.

Your obedient Servant,
JAMES A. YOUL.

Mr. G. SPRIGG,
    Secretary Acclimatization Society.

(Reply to Foreign Correspondents respecting Consignments.)

LONDON, 8th Oct., 1866.

Messrs. BEVERIDGE & GOODALL,
    Buenos Ayres.

DEAR SIRS,—I beg to acknowledge receipt of your favour of 25th August, and note contents, which are satisfactory. I shall also now reply more fully to your favour of 22nd July than I could do, for want of time, so close upon the departure of last mail.

The result of case No. 130, per *Courier*, does not surprise me, as there were in it articles of a second-rate character, sent merely by way of experiment, and which I shall not repeat, confining myself in future to superior goods.

The errors I had complained of per *Parilla* and *Courier* are now satisfactorily explained, and I have passed the sum advised, viz. $3,059, to your debit, as your share of the loss for wrong declaration. I hope our future transactions will make up for this annoyance and loss to both of us.

I shall feel obliged by your closing as speedily as

possible the balances of old shipments, such as the following :—

No. 4, per *Parilla ;* No. 9, per *Maria ;* and No. 15, per *Ignis Fatuus.* I should also esteem it a favour if you would send me, per return mail, an account current to date, to see that our books agree. Annexed I beg to hand you B/L and Invoice of ten cases of cutlery and soft goods, and one case of electro-plated goods, per *Witch of the Seas,* which I trust will reach you promptly, and meet with ready sale. I shall send you another lot of ale and wine about December. Can you do nothing in Monte Video ? I fear not, as the cases I sent you to that port per *Sindbad* you had transhipped on to Buenos Ayres. I shall be glad to receive the list furnished by your inland customers, as a guide to shipments suited for Paraguay and the interior States.

I am, dear Sirs, yours truly,

J. HARWOOD.

(Instructions for Claim for Loss of Goods Insured.)

DEAR SIR,—I send you the necessary papers for a claim per *Glenark,* which you had insured for me. Shall I make out the claim, or will you ? I have only claimed for £60, although the certificate states that the goods would have been worth £125 sound value.

Yours truly,

RICHARD JOHNSTON.

D. R. B.
28/30.

3 cases of Perfumery insured for............ £80
Realized at auction............................... 20
                                                                  ———
                                               Loss ... £60
Paid for certificate of damage.................. 2
    „   „   of sound value............ 2

(Application for Bill of Lading.)

LIVERPOOL, *April 24th*, 1865.

P. L. SIMMONDS, Esq.

DEAR SIR,—Referring to your telegram of 21st inst., we shall feel obliged by your handing us the Bill of Lading for the cases referred to, which goes forward to Dublin to-day.   Account for freight, &c., will follow to-morrow.

We are, dear Sir,
Yours truly,
FLETCHER & PARR,
per J. W.

(Letter with Bills of Lading.)

(Enclosures.)

DUBLIN, *20th April*, 1865.

DEAR SIR,—Enclosed I beg to hand letter received this day from Messrs. W. Gray & Co., respecting the arrival of goods from Port Natal, consigned to us, as per Bills of

Lading herewith, which would you be kind enough to endorse for us, and hand to them, and oblige

Yours faithfully,

C. E. BAGOT,

Sec. Exec. Committee.

P. L. SIMMONDS, Esq.

(From Shipping Agents.)

COLONIAL CHAMBERS, CRUTCHED FRIARS,

21st June, 1865.

P. L. SIMMONDS, Esq.

DEAR SIR,—Enclosed we beg to hand you B/L for shipments per last steamer to Oporto.

We have Mr. Abatt's case of maps, and Mr. Feyer's case of cider here in the office, and have this morning received advice of the despatch of two cases from the Imperial Iron Tube Co., Birmingham, to our address. Are these goods to go on to Oporto at once ?

We are, dear Sir,

Yours very truly

, W. H. IVENS & SON,

per GEO. WEAVER.

1 Enclosure.

(Instructions to Shipping Agent.)

LONDON, *June*, 1865.

Messrs. CHINNERY & Co.

GENTLEMEN,—I expect from Paris immediately the following cases :—

R. W. & Co., 297 to 307, to be shipped (with a few

British cases ready in a day or two) per first vessel for Adelaide.   Consignees, Ripley, Webb, & Co.   Amount of insurance in my next.

R. F. & Co., 277-81 per first vessel to Bombay.   Consigned to Messrs. Frith & Co.   Insurance £100.

W. D. M. 282-96, per first vessel for Sydney.   B/L to order.   Insurance £180.

73 in a diamond to be claimed by delivery, Fraser.

A. J. & Co., 308.   Grey & Coles. $\boxed{\text{E A}}$ 309.

J. S. & Co., 310, by delivery.   B V 325 delivery. Yates & Co.

I have no B/L for K. & B. 1, per *Columbia*, shipped since the 21st May.

Will you please re-mark the cases B H B 1/3 as follows : K. & Co. 1/3, and ship them per first vessel for Wellington, N. Z.   Consignees, Messrs. Knill & Co., merchants. Insurance £110.

Your prompt attention and reply will oblige

Your obedient Servant,

J. SIDNEY.

(Enquiry as to Ships Sailing.)

LONDON, *Sept.*, 1866.

Mr. TAMPLIN, Liverpool.

SIR,—Please inform me by return what is the first ship, sailing or steam, on the berth for Santander, and what are the current rates of freight, both for measurement goods and dead weight.

W. WIGMORE.

(Advice of Transmission of Goods for Foreign Shipment.)

Messrs. HORSFALL & Co.,
          Liverpool.

GENTLEMEN,—I have sent by Chaplin & Horne this day 1 case of British goods marked R S in diamond 7, for Mr. Silberman, Halifax, N. S. You will also receive 1 case of French goods same mark, No. 6, from my agents, Messrs. Chinnery, Johnson, & Co., 67, Lower Thames Street, which I trust will arrive in time to be shipped according to Mr. Silberman's instructions.

I am, Gentlemen,
    Your obedient Servant,
          T. D. DENNIS.

———

(The same.)

Mr. ELLISON, Liverpool.

DEAR SIR,—I have sent by Chaplin & Horne to-day seven cases to be forwarded by steamer to Santander. Enclosed are Consul's particulars in duplicate, one of which please send by the ship to Santander. Also pay freight and all charges to Santander, and insure for sum of £150.

I am, dear Sir,
    Yours truly,
          W. MOUNCEY.

(Enclosure.)

CONSULAR PARTICULARS of Seven Cases marked PL.S,
68/72, consigned to Don Sevana & Co., Santander.

No.	Gross Wt. of case in Spanish.		Nett Wt. of Contents.		Quantity.	English Name.	Spanish Name.
	arr.	lb.	arr.	lb.			
68	11	22	8	0		Perfumery	Perfumaria.
69	5	7	3	18		Linen	Lienzo.
70	6	23	2	12		Steel	Acero.
			0	9¾		Vegetable Wax.	Cera vegetal.
			0	19½		Orris - Root Powder.	Raiz de Ireos de Florencia
			0	9¾		Tonquin - Bean Powder.	Fabas de Tonka molidao.
			0	9¾		Powdered Benzoin.	Benjui (polvos de).
71	11	12	6	0		Apothecary's Wares.	Droga.
72	13	15	6	11		Stearine Candles	Candela.
73	6	23	3	11	50	Ladies' Combs..	Peines por las Senoras.
						Hair Brushes ..	Bruza para limpiar el caballo.
74	6	10	2	2		Perfumery	Perfumaria.
			0	23	4 dz.	Horse - Hair Frizzettes.	Rulos de cerda.
			0	1½	6 yards	Alpaca........	Alpaca.
			0	4¼		Tinfoil Paper ..	Papel metalico.
			0	4½		Invoices, Envelopes and Letter-paper.	Impresos, Papel de carta y sobres.
			0	1		Sewing Cotton..	Algodon para coser.
			4 ounces			Bracelets	Brazalete de oro y terceopelo.
			10 „			Lady's Hat....	Sombrero de Senora.

(Objections as to Insurance.)

Messrs. CHINNERY & Co.

DEAR SIRS,—My instructions having been quite positive for insurance "free of all risks," I beg to inform you that I decline the insurance you have effected against my orders, and hold you responsible.   I prefer no insurance at all to that with the limitation of "free of average."

I shall have a case ready in a day or two for Santander.

Yours truly,
J. HAYTHORN.

(Particulars for Shipping Agent.)

Mr. JOSEPH HARRIS,
Lower Thames Street.

SIR,—Enclosed I hand you B/L for one case curiosities, which please forward to Mr. Seghers, 2, Rue des Boulevards, au Coin de la rue de Berlin, Paris. Charges forward.   You will also find a receipt for the freight, which is stated not to be paid on the B/L, but was paid subsequently.

I expect, from Paris by steamer, case E R M for home consumption.   751

Contents.

Silk net, value	£24
Brushes	8
Printed paper............... by weight.	
Essential Oil .... Free.	

Please let me have the case as soon as possible.

Your obedient Servant,
JOHN HAYDON.

(Complaint of Want of Instructions, and Application for Money.)

LONDON, 20*th June*, 1865.

Messrs. HAILES, THOMSON, & Co.,
   Leeds.

GENTLEMEN,—I confirm my letter of the 12th inst.,
and am rather surprised at your not replying to the same
as requested. It seems that I am not likely to be more
fortunate with your house in Leeds in obtaining an
answer than I have been with your London branch.

I once more request you will let me know, per return
of post, by what vessel you wish me to ship those cases
for Sydney, which have been so long ready, and beg you
will at the same time enclose a cheque for the amount of
your account, £58. 11*s.* 6*d.*, which is fully due.

    I remain
     Your obedient Servant,
      JAMES GOWER.

(Application for Shipping Note.)

June 20*th*, 1865.

Mr. NIXON GOWER,
   Basinghall Street.

SIR,—I have now ready 2 cases of wine marked R & H
             M
for Messrs. Robinson & Hartley, Melbourne, for which
please to send a shipping note, and oblige

    Sir,
     Your obedient Servant,
      Pro HOWE & SON,
       J. MACINNES.

(Correspondence with Shipping Agents.)

June 30th, 1856.

Messrs. CHINNERY & Co.

GENTLEMEN,—Please do not wait any longer, but ship per first vessel the case for Messrs. Young & Co. Also send per return your account of charges since the beginning of the month.

Yours truly,

T. CUTLER.

Messrs. CHEFFIN BROS.

DEAR SIRS,—I beg to enclose you a claim from Mr. Elkington for Fifty Pounds for short shipment of two cases containing Photographic chemicals and appliances which I had undertaken to get shipped for him last February, and for which I received from you B/Lading duly signed by the captain.

Your early attention to this matter will oblige, and in the meanwhile I request you will return me the cases here, as it appears it is of no use sending them on now

I remain, dear Sirs,
Yours truly,

JOHN TOMKINS.

Messrs. H. WARD & Co.

GENTLEMEN,—Please to receive 1 case marked D 1, to be consigned to Mr. G. D. Witte, Lubeck, *vià* Hamburg steamer, with instructions to forward to Messrs. Dereham & Co., St. Petersburg. All charges on.

Declaration.

	WEIGHT.	
	Net.	Gross.
Silk gloves ....7 lb.		27 lb.

Value £15.

Yours truly,

T. KIRKMAN.

(Particulars and Instructions to Shipping Agents.)

GENTLEMEN,—Enclosed are particulars of ten cases for St. Petersburg, all charges to be sent on, and of three cases for Boston, America, the whole of which have been sent to the Docks this morning. Let me have Bills of Lading as soon as signed, for transmission.

Yours truly,

E. PULLAN.

Particulars of 3 cases for Boston marked L & R 3/5
                                       B

3.	160 lb. Perfumed Soap, sample stand £7	13	8
4.	160 lb. Perfumed Soap, 12 sample bottles Perfumery ....} 7	13	8
5.	157 lb. Perfumed Soap 5	15	3

Particulars of Ten Cases, marked T R C. 1/10, to be sent by steamer to Madame T. R. Capucin, St. Petersburg.

No. of Case.	Gross Weight of Cases	Weight of Contents. Gross.	Weight of Contents. Net.	Quantity.	Value.	Definition.
	lb.	lb. oz.	lb. oz.		£. s.	
1	373		340 0		13 0	Savon parfumé.
2	289		259 0		11 10	,, ,,
3	367		339 0		14 10	,, ,,
4	279	50 0	25 0	25 doz.		Boîtes d'écorce de bois.
			102 0		5 0	Verrerie.
			3 14			Produits chimiques.
5	243		151 0		0 10	Faïence.
			7 0			Tableau.
			2 0			Cartes.
6	216		56 0		12 0	Savon mou parfumé.
			101 8			Savon parfumé.
7	181		120 0		1 0	Faïence.
8	135		20 0			Pommade parfumée.
		12 12	9 0			Parfumerie.
			36 0	8 doz.	20 10	Verrerie en étuis de bois.
			7 0			Tableau.
9	146	14 10	12 0	6 tins	18 0	Eau de Senteur.
			74 0	16 doz.		Boîtes d'écorce de bois.
10	151	9 0	5 8	1 jar		Pommade parfumée.
		32 8	28 5	6 tins		,, ,,
		6 14	3 0	2 ,,	20 0	Poudre parfumée.
		73 0	70 0			Poudre non parfumée.
			8 0			Etiquettes et Imprimes.

Messrs. J. R. McCracken & Co.

Gentlemen,—Please send to-morrow for 1 case F R 38/4 to be forwarded per steamer to Rotterdam, care of P. Pitman & Co.; thence in bond to Amsterdam.

Contents.

106 lb. Perfumed Soap.

12 doz. Perfumery.

Value £10. 16*s.*

Charges all forward.

Yours respectfully,

M. KENT.

(Letter to Shipping Agents.)

LONDON, *August,* 1866.

GENTLEMEN,—Will you look out for the arrival of the *Runnymede,* which has 2 chests of tea on board for me, and when the vessel arrives, re-ship the tea in bond to my house in Boulogne?

Enclosed is B/L from Baltimore. Contents, essential oil, free, for home consumption; also order for 25 bales Cuscus root. I am in doubt if these are not forfeitable. At all events, inquire what rent and charges are due, and I will let you know whether to take them or leave them, the value being probably scarce worth the warehouse rent.

Yours truly,

PHILIP JENKINS.

(Instructions to effect Insurance.)

Mr. JACKSON.

DEAR SIR,—Please insure, free of particular average, the following :—

SH 8/9   2 cases, per *Emperor,* Madras, value... £50

PB 318/19 2 „   „ *Windermere,* Hobart Town 40

ER 8/11	4 cases, per *Bury St. Edmund's,* Mauritius	} £70	
SH 272/6 ...	5 „ „ *Sir R. Sale,* Madras...	90	
MLC 328/31...	4 „ „ *Wentworth,* Calcutta	80	
WCY 1/3 & 54/5	} 5 „ „ *Evening Star,* Otago	80	
VDM 282/96 & 6/10	} 20 „ „ *Lochiel,* Sydney	250	
RWC 1/4 & 297/307	} 15 „ „ { *Corsair's Bride,* Adelaide..................	180	
H W 20–307	2 „ „ *Scawfell,* Hong Kong	50	
VD 389/95 & 11/16	} 14 „ „ *Summer Cloud,* Sydney	200	

Yours truly,

E. GIBSON.

(Advice of Shipment, and apology for unexecuted order.)

LONDON, 14*th Aug.*

Mr. WATSON, Cape Town.

DEAR SIR,—I confirm my last of 19th July, and have now the pleasure of handing you Invoice and B/L of your order for Paris goods, which I forwarded as directed by mail steamer. I send you an invoice without discount, as requested.

I received by last mail your favour of 15th June, and immediately referred to your correspondence, when I found, to my utter surprise, that the order for glass, &c., you sent in your letter of the 15th January, had, by some unaccountable neglect, been overlooked, your letter having been put away without the order being copied.

Being absent myself at the time of its arrival, the omission rests with my entering clerk, for whose neglect

I must apologize. I have now given out the order for execution, and you may depend upon the cases being forwarded by a fast ship by the end of this month.

I trust you will suffer no inconvenience from this delay, for unfortunately late advices report that business was dull in the Cape Colony, and, moreover, they will reach your market in the busy season.

You may depend upon your future orders being attended to with promptitude and precision. This is the first time such an omission has occurred since I have been in business, and I will take care that it is the last.

I remain,
Yours truly,
J. GRIERSON.

BUSINESS LETTERS ON INTERNATIONAL EXHIBITION MATTERS.

—◆◆—

26th April, 1862.

DEAR SIR,—I called to see you this afternoon, but found you had left for the day. The collection we had prepared from West Africa, the Portuguese Government have insisted on exhibiting themselves. We have, however, a very fine collection of fibrous grass from Spain, in its raw state, and in the different stages up to paper, showing the process of its manufacture. Could you assist us in obtaining a small space for this? we should only require three or four feet, I should think. The British Industrial Department would be the best place for it. Waiting to hear from you at your early convenience,

I am, Sir,
Yours very faithfully,

P. L. SIMMONDS, Esq.   J. M. LOZANO.

9, FRIDAY STREET, CHEAPSIDE, LONDON, E.C.,
8th March, 1865.

P. L. SIMMONDS, Esq.,
    Interdational Exhibition,
        Dublin.

SIR,—Our friend Mr. A. W. Faber, of Stein, in Bavaria, manufacturer of pencils, school slates, &c.,

I

having applied for space in the Dublin Exhibition through your agent at Frankfort-on-the-Maine, Mr. Peter Bender, sent off a few days ago a collection of his different manufactures, worthy of his world-wide reputation.

To his surprise he has just received a telegram from Mr. Bender: "Slates cannot be admitted;" and we have been requested to seek an explanation at headquarters.

If school slates are excluded from the Exhibition for some mysterious reason, Mr. Faber would be compelled to withdraw the whole of his collection, which now forms a complete illustration of what the largest manufactory in the world produces in the auxiliaries of art and education.

We are inclined to believe that there is a ridiculous mistake somewhere, and hazard the suggestion that Mr. Faber's slates have been confounded with *roof* slates, or other building materials. Any how, Mr. Faber is anxious to know the decision of your Committee, and we shall be glad soon to hear from you on this subject.

We avail ourselves of this opportunity to inquire, on behalf of our friends the Hoerder Steel and Iron Works in Westphalia, whether your flooring is strong enough to bear a weight of about 35 tons spread over a surface of 40 × 16 feet.

They will have an immense contribution of steel plates, tyres, axles, wheels, &c., which, we believe, will be unique of its kind.

We are, Sir,
Yours truly,
HEINTZMANN & ROCHUSSEN.

BRITISH AND NORTH AMERICAN ROYAL MAIL STEAM PACKET
COMPANY,
Office—8, WATER STREET, LIVERPOOL,

27th April, 1865.

P. L. SIMMONDS, Esq.,
International Exhibition,
Dublin.

DEAR SIR,—We beg to inform you that we yesterday shipped per City of Dublin Steam Company, 19 packages, which arrived per R.M.S. *Asia ;* 18 addressed Rev. Dr. Honeyman, Dublin Exhibition, and one addressed John D. Nash, Dublin Exhibition. They are under charge of the Customs as before, and we trust they will arrive all right.

Yours truly,
D. & C. MAC IVER.

LEICESTER CHAMBER OF COMMERCE.
OFFICE—24, FRIAR LANE,

1st September, 1864.

MY LORD,—I am desired by the Worshipful the Mayor of Leicester to acknowledge the receipt of a circular letter signed by your Lordship, requesting his assistance as Chief Magistrate, to promote the prosperity of the International Exhibition to be held next year in Dublin.

The Mayor has handed this letter to the Directors of the Chamber of Commerce for consideration, believing that to be the course most likely to forward the object your Lordship has in view.

I shall have the honour of submitting the question to the Directors in a few days.

> I have the honour to be, my Lord,
> Your Lordship's most obedient Servant,
> T. A. WYKES,
> Secretary.

‑ The Rt. Hon. the LORD MAYOR OF DUBLIN.

> GLOUCESTERSHIRE PUBLIC OFFICES, TEWKESBURY,
> *August* 29*th*, 1864.

MY LORD MAYOR,—I have duly received your Lordship's circular, together with the resolution of the Committee of Advice; and I have the satisfaction to inform your Lordship that the Town Council of this Borough, with the assistance of its most respectable inhabitants, will most readily co-operate with your Committee; and that a Sub-Committee will be immediately formed, of which I shall act as Hon. Secretary.

> I have the honour to be,
> My Lord Mayor,
> Fathfully your Servant,
> JAMES HITCH,
> Mayor.

To the LORD MAYOR,
Dublin

LONDON, *April 10th*, 1865.

DEAR SIR,—In reply to your inquiry of the 9th inst., the dimensions of the model are 7 ft. 9 in. × 4 ft. 9 in., and height 5 ft. 3 in.

It will be delivered at the Dublin Steam Wharf to-morrow; the steamer will start for Dublin on Wednesday morning.

Of course we insure the sea risk; but as respects insurance against fire, we shall be glad to learn by return whether that is provided for by the managers of the Exhibition. Our estimate of the value of the model is £200, for which we shall take out a policy, if not provided for on your side.

We are much obliged by your attention in procuring a favourable site, and remain, dear Sir,

Yours truly,

ROBT. FAUNTLEROY & Co.,

P. L. SIMMONDS, Esq.　　　Per Thomas Day.

LONDON, *April 1st*, 1865.

DEAR SIR,—The slab of malachite was forwarded yesterday for this day's steamer, addressed to you at the Exhibition, Dublin, and I hope will arrive safely.

Perhaps you will kindly enter it as from the " Peak Downs Copper Mines," Queensland, Australia, exhibited by W. Mort, 155, Fenchurch Street, London.

I am, dear Sir,

Yours faithfully,

P. L. SIMMONDS, Esq.　　　W. MORT.

LONDON, E.C., 31*st March*, 1865.

DEAR SIR,—As it will not look well for my country to be unrepresented at the Dublin Exhibition, it is my intention to exhibit a fine display of Maltese lace and filigree work. I cannot undertake anything in the stonework line.

I have already written to Malta · to say that I will undertake to exhibit the goods, and be responsible for them, and also pay expenses.

Will you kindly let me know how much room you can allot for the Malta Court, and how far you can assist me, so that I may send Mr. Roydhouse to make the necessary preparations and arrangements?

> I remain, dear Sir,
> Yours very truly,
> ALFRED FERRO.

THE ORIENTAL COMMERCIAL COMPANY (LIMITED),
31, THREADNEEDLE STREET, LONDON, E.C.,
January 10*th*, 1865.

To P. L. SIMMONDS, Esq.,
Superintendent,
Dublin International Exhibition.

SIR,—With reference to the request conveyed in your note under date of the 7th, which we received this morning, and have now the honour to acknowledge, we beg leave to state that we will communicate on the subject by the earliest respective mails, with our various

correspondents, soliciting their particular attention to
the matter, and requesting them, if possible, to contribute
suitable specimens of produce and manufactures, or works
of art, and to enable us to give you timely advice of any
packages coming forward.

I am, Sir,
Your obedient Servant,
DEMETRIO PAPPE,
Manager.

THE ORIENTAL COMMERCIAL COMPANY (LIMITED),
31, THREADNEEDLE STREET, LONDON, E.C.,
January 12th, 1865.

To P. L. SIMMONDS, Esq.

SIR,—We have duly received the parcel of printed
documents respecting the Exhibition with which you
favour us.

By this day's mail we have communicated on the
subject with all our agents in Greece and the Levant.

On Monday we will send instructions to have advertisements published in all the local papers, inviting attention to the matter, and the contribution of specimens. And
immediately upon any movement being signified to us,
we will appoint some competent person or persons to
superintend the collection and despatch of such articles
as may be tendered to our agents.

In the like sense we communicate by each conveyance
offering, to our different correspondents abroad, and we
trust these measures will bring about results satisfactory
to the Council and Committee of the undertaking, and

that we may be of service in promoting a movement which is proved by all experience, as well as believed on principle, to be of the highest utility to industry and progress throughout the world.

> I am, Sir,
> Your obedient Servant,
> DEMETRIO PAPPL,
> Manager.

LIVERPOOL, *22nd March,* 1865.

P. L. SIMMONDS, Esq.

SIR,—Having been appointed the representative of Victoria (Australia), to look after the goods to be exhibited at Dublin, I beg to inquire the particulars of the space which has been allotted. The Melbourne Committee have applied for 1,500 superficial feet of floor-space. The goods will arrive by the steamer *Great Britain* about the end of May, and I am anxious to make all arrangements respecting them beforehand, so as to lose no time in getting them into their place.

> I am, Sir,
> Yours respectfully,
> TYNDALL BRIGHT.

Dec. 21, 1864.

SIR,—You would oblige me by letting me know if an inlaid table of Jamaica woods can be shown in the Colonial Department at the forthcoming Exhibition.

Its history is briefly this :—During the time of the Exhibition in 1862 I was residing in Jamaica, and I read in the *Daily Telegraph* an account of two tables of Jamaica manufacture, which seemed to attract great attention. I spoke to the manufacturers in Kingston, Jamaica, and learned from them that these were two of their smaller-sized tables, which Governor Darling had brought over with him. I subsequently learned that the Governor had sold them at a very considerable advance on cost price. When leaving the island, I found that the freight charged on my heavy baggage was considerable, and forgetting the proverb about the shoemaker and his last, I resolved to speculate in a table. I ordered one of the largest and handsomest, and it duly arrived in this country. But I have totally failed in getting it exhibited in any of the West End shops in London. I candidly apprise you that my object is to get it sold ; but as it really affords a good specimen of Jamaica woods and colonial manufacture, it may not be undeserving of a place in your collection.

Awaiting your reply,

I have the honour to be, Sir,

Your faithful Servant,

P. S. WILTON.

P. L. SIMMONDS, Esq.

2, BROAD STREET BUILDINGS,

LONDON, 28th November, 1864.

SIR,—I have the honour to acknowledge the receipt of your letter of 26th inst., on the subject of the International Exhibition which is to be held in Dublin next year.

I hasten to inform you that I have already received a despatch from the Imperial Government stating that it has made known to the subjects of His Imperial Majesty the Sultan, that an International Exhibition would be held in Dublin, and invited them to contribute specimens of their agricultural and industrial products; and instructing me to appoint an employé of the Embassy to take charge of whatever objects may be collected for exhibition.

Until the definitive appointment of the employé of the Embassy, I have requested Mr. Gadban, the Consul-General of the Sublime Porte at London, to take charge of all articles intended to be exhibited, which may in the meanwhile be sent to this country.

I shall, however, have much pleasure in transmitting to the Imperial Government a copy of your letter, and the papers therein referred to, and in strongly recommending your suggestions to its favourable consideration.

I have the honour to be, Sir,
Your obedient Servant,
C. MUSSURUS.

C. E. BAGOT, Esq.

HAMBURG, 21st January, 1865.

P. L. SIMMONDS, Esq.

DEAR SIR,—We had yesterday the pleasure of receiving the prospectus of the Dublin International Exhibition for this year; and seeing it to have been despatched on your behalf, we sincerely beg to thank you for this token of remembrance.

The purpose of writing you to-day is to tell you that our friend the well-known Mr. H. F. C. Rampendahl, carver in ivory, &c., feels inclined to exhibit at Dublin ; but remembering the heavy expense and annoyances of the Exhibition in London, he wants first to find some individual or respectable firm at Dublin, to whom he could safely trust his valuable articles, and to whom he would pay a certain fixed per-centage, to include receiving the goods, putting them up in the Exhibition, attending to, and selling them, remitting the proceeds, re-packing the articles not sold, and sending them back to Hamburg ; in fact, including all and every charge and expense from the moment the goods are landed from the steamer until they are reshipped. The freight is, however, to be paid by Mr. Rampendahl, and not to be included in the above per-centage. You will oblige us by stating whether any and what arrangements were made with the steamers to carry the goods over to Dublin at a reduction of the ordinary freight.

As you, dear Sir, are most likely well acquainted with parties undertaking the sort of business referred to above, we hope you will be able to name for Mr. Rampendahl a suitable and reliable person.

Any other particulars you think of interest to Mr. Rampendahl will be received with thanks.

We remain, dear Sir,

Yours faithfully

W. A. LEPPER & Co.

CROSBY HOUSE, LONDON, E.C.,

26th January, 1865.

P. L. SIMMONDS, Esq.

DEAR SIR,—We are duly in receipt of your favour of yesterday, and as we are writing to our houses at the Cape and Natal by this evening's mail, we will put the subject prominently before them.

We are sorry the notice is so short ; but our friends, no doubt, will press the subject as much as possible, on account of the Exhibition opening so early as the 9th May.

Yours truly,

GOODLIFFE & SMART.

101, HIGH STREET, PORTSMOUTH,

June 18*th,* 1865.

DEAR SIR,—We are obliged by your favour of yesterday's date, and enclose you herewith the notice we received of the space which we applied for in the Oporto Exhibition, having been allotted to us.

We purpose to exhibit there a case of Engraved Crystal-work and other jewellery, mounted as brooches, &c., with a view of selling them, or obtaining orders therefrom.

We should therefore esteem it a favour if you would inform us if you think it advisable for us to send the case of goods as we had originally intended, and if you can recommend us any *responsible* and first-rate man of business at Oporto, who would undertake the charge of our case, and sell or obtain orders for us on commission.

Will you also kindly inform us what is the latest date to forward the goods?

Apologizing for thus troubling you, which we have been induced to do on the introduction of our mutual friend Mr. Henry Hollingsworth, and awaiting favour of reply,

We are, dear Sir,

Yours faithfully,

E. & E. EMANUEL.

P. L. SIMMONDS, Esq.,
    London Superintendent
        of the Portuguese Exhibition,
           John Street, Adelphi.

101, HIGH STREET, PORTSMOUTH,

June 20*th*, 1865.

DEAR SIR,—We are obliged by your explanatory letter of yesterday's date. We enclose form of demand for space filled up as requested.

We should be glad if you would place Mr. Maurice in communication with us as regards undertaking our agency at Oporto. We understand from your letter that he is now in England, and if so, Mr. E. would call on him in town, and endeavour to arrange terms, &c.

The only inquiry we have now unanswered is as regards the latest date for shipment, as we do not know when the Exhibition is to open and when to close. We await information hereon from your shipping agents, and a communication from Mr. Maurice.

With many thanks, we are,

Dear Sir,
Yours faithfully,
E. & E. EMANUEL.

P. L. SIMMONDS, Esq.

SHEFFIELD, 22nd June, 1865.

P. L. SIMMONDS, Esq., London.

SIR,—Referring to our application of 14th, for an extension of the space granted to us previously in the Oporto Crystal· Palace, we should be very glad to learn by return that it has been successful, as we are venturing to proceed with the preparation of our show cases, in the hope that such may be the case.

We remain, Sir,
Yours very truly,
JOHN KENYON & Co.

LIVERPOOL, 26th Feb. 1866

P. L. SIMMONDS, Esq.,
            Exhibition Palace,
                  Dublin.

DEAR SIR,—I should feel obliged if you would let me know how soon the Medals and Certificates of Honourable

Mention awarded to the Exhibitors in the Victorian Department can be forwarded here, as I fear that not only will the Exhibitors be getting anxious for their receipt, but that the value of the awards will be much depreciated by further delay.

Hoping you will kindly use your influence in facilitating their early despatch,

I remain, dear Sir,

Yours faithfully,

TYNDALL BRIGHT.

JERSEY, *May* 23, 1865.

SIR,—We are favoured with a letter from Mr. Wm. Boulton, of Redditch, enclosing your note to him on the subject of our preserves for the Dublin Exhibition.

We hasten to avail ourselves of your kind permission, to send a small case of them to your address, say

1 6-lb. tin Preserved fresh Salmon.
1 1-lb. „   „   „
2 1-lb. tins   „   fresh Lobster.
2   „   „   Cod tongues.

The last are a new description of preserve, and not known in commerce. They are considered a great delicacy, are generally served fried in butter, well browned, and require only ten minutes' cooking.

The above have been preserved at our establishments in Newfoundland.

We also send

         1 tin Oysters, a pint.

         1   „   „ $\frac{1}{2}$ pint.

These have been preserved at our factory in this island.

We beg to request the favour of your placing these few articles in as favourable a position as you can afford, so as to bring them under the notice of visitors and others interested.

Trusting that they may meet with the favourable consideration of the jurors,

             We are, Sir,

               Yours obediently,

      Pro DE GRUCHY, RENOUF, CLEMENT, & Co.,

                     P. L. DE GRUCHY.

P. L. SIMMONDS, Esq.,

      Colonial Superintendent,

           The Exhibition Palace, Dublin.

THE COTTON PLANTATION COMPANY OF NATAL (LIMITED),

                 LONDON, *May 9th,* 1865.

P. L. SIMMONDS, Esq.,

      Dublin Exhibition.

DEAR SIR,—I have this day forwarded to you a small box containing three samples of cotton grown in Natal, with labels upon them, describing each sample, enclosed in glass tube bottles, which I hope you will find suitable for your purpose.

I presume you have other labels to put on the bottles.

I have therefore put on temporary ones only, supposing you require some uniformity in the labels.

Hoping they will reach you safely,

I am, dear Sir,

Yours truly,

G. R. HAYWOOD,

Secretary.

June 6th, 1865.

SIR,—Having had some little business in London, I was deputed by Messrs. John Kenyon & Co., of Sheffield, to call on you relative to the Portuguese Exhibition.

Messrs. John Kenyon & Co., my employers, have had space allotted to them to exhibit, and I have the getting up of the affair.

The space allotted to us, 12 ft. long, we propose to fill with a vertical case 12 ft. long, 7 ft. high, and 6 to 12 inches deep ; also a horizontal case, 12 ft. long, 3½ ft. wide, and 12 in. deep. Will these two cases stand together, something like this sketch, the vertical over the horizontal case ?

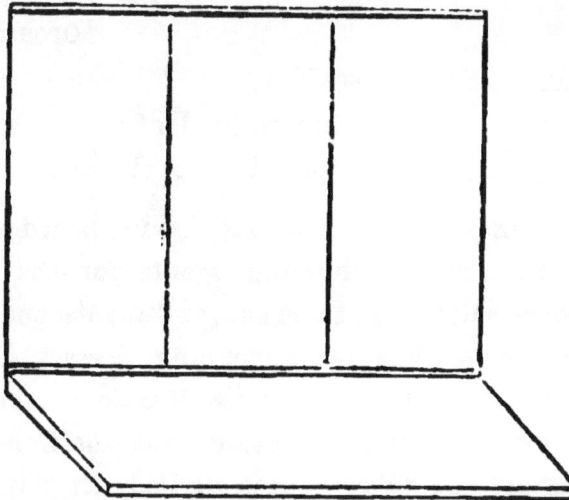

Supposing each are separate from the other, will the upright case stand against a wall ?

We want the vertical case to stand about 30 inches above the floor, if separate from the other. Will the Exhibition authorities provide proper and efficient support for the case at that height from the floor, or shall we have to do that?

Will you please oblige by answers to the above queries, addressed to

Your obedient Servant,
J. WILDE,
Messrs. J. Kenyon & Co., Sheffield.

P. L. SIMMONDS, Esq.

OPORTO, 8th June, 1865.

P. L. SIMMONDS, Esq.,
　　　London Superintendent,
　　　　　Society of Arts, London.

DEAR SIR,—Yesterday, having heard of the unfortunate failure of the shipping agents for the Exhibition, I at once called on Mr. Allen, and mentioned the case to him, at same time recommending Messrs. Cheffins Brothers to him, as persons very well able to take charge of the business. Mr. Allen said that the Committee could not undertake to guarantee anybody as shipping agents, but that I had better at once telegraph Messrs. Cheffins Brothers, as well as yourself, so that no time might be lost in sending circulars round to all those persons that are going to send goods for exhibition. I hope you have made arrangements with the above house, as I am certain you will find they will give every attention and assistance to your important duties, as also to the interests of the exhibitors.

I am,
Yours truly,
AUG. J. SHORE.

(Application for Employment.)

EVESHAM, *July 3rd*, 1865.

SIR,—As you are interested in the Oporto Exhibition, I thought it just possible you might have inquiries for a person conversant with languages.

If so, I beg to say I have a son now at Cologne, who has been exhibiting there and at Stettin, for Mr. T. Bond, of Manchester, whose engagement terminates with the Cologne show.

He is well up in German, almost equal to a native; has resided in Paris, and can speak French; has also some knowledge of Spanish. He attended the Hamburg show in '63 for Mr. Bond, and carried on a branch establishment there for him, until the breaking out of the Danish war.

He has been accustomed to the Ironmongery trade. I can strongly recommend him, should you hear of an opening.

Trusting you will excuse this liberty,

I am, Sir,
Yours obediently,
P. L. SIMMONDS, Esq.   JOHN STONE.

5, York Street, Liverpool,
19*th July*, 1865.

Sir,—We should be inclined to send a couple of cases, about four cubic feet each, of our preparations to the Portuguese Exhibition, if you would oblige us with particulars. They are goods largely consumed in our colonies. The principal is refined table salt, of which we export about 300 cases per week, and scouring or polishing powder, in which we have a large export business.

We are, Sir,
Your obedient Servants,
John Pearson & Co.

P. L. Simmonds, Esq.

Park Lane, Leeds,
July 20*th*, 1865.

P. L. Simmonds, Esq., London.

Dear Sir,—On the 26th June I had my case ready for delivery to the Midland Railway Company, to take to London, and addressed to the care of Messrs. W. H. Ivens & Son, for shipment to Oporto. When I received a letter from Messrs. Cheffins Brothers informing me that they had been appointed by you "the forwarding Agents," and that I was to inform them "the space and number of packages required to be forwarded." This I did by return of post; but up to the present moment I have not received any reply. I have this day forwarded per Midland Rail, the package to the address given

by them (in London), and hope it will be right. I
thought it quite unsafe to delay keeping back the case
any longer. Thanking you for your kindness,

I remain, dear Sir,
Faithfully yours,
E. B. STEELE.

BELFAST, *June 29th*, 1865.

P. L. SIMMONDS, Esq., London.

SIR,—We have the honour to enclose you a " demand
for space " in the Portuguese International Exhibition,
at the same time apologizing for being so late; but we
understood that our Paris house (who have made arrangements to exhibit their French manufactures) had done all
the needful for us; and only learn now that they have
not done so.

As we have so little time, we shall feel much obliged
if you will let us know, as early as possible, if our request
for space is complied with; and, the *latest date* up to
which they will receive our goods.

We are, Sir,
Yours respectfully,
H. GUYNET & Co.

BRIDGWATER, *July 7th*, 1865.

P. L. SIMMONDS, Esq.

SIR,—Having made inquiries some time since, as to
whether my Cask-cleansing Machine would be useful, or

likely to be adopted in Portugal, and receiving replies in the negative, I had given up the idea of exhibiting there.

Your conversation with Mr. Parkinson, my attendant in the Dublin Exhibition, has, however, placed the matter in a new light.   If you will kindly favour me with any particulars of the intended Exhibition, I will again consider the matter, and shall feel particularly obliged by replies to the following questions, viz. :—

1. The cost of machine to Oporto, weight about 9 cwt. (say half a ton).

2. Commission intended to be charged by the person who intends to be at the Exhibition, for taking charge of the machine, and seeing that it is kept in clean order, oiled, &c.

3. Is the person known to you as one who will see that the duties entered upon will be *fully carried out ?*

4. At what time should the machine be delivered in London ?

5. Is it your opinion that a machine of this character *is* required in Portugal ?

You will pardon me asking so many questions, but I am desirous of not spending money in this matter, unless they have use for the machines in Portugal.

I am, Sir,
Yours truly,
W. ROBINSON.

BOLTON, *Aug. 15th,* 1865.

DEAR SIR,—I beg to inform you that our safe has been sent to-day to Messrs. Chiffins Bros. I have another to send, but it is not quite ready. Have the kindness to inform me if it will be possible to get it into the Exhibition after it (the Exhibition) is opened, and oblige

Yours faithfully,
SAMUEL CHATWOOD.

P. L. SIMMONDS, Esq.

P.S.—Our London agents, Messrs. Letts, Son, & Co., are willing to allow us space sufficient for our purpose out of their allotment; *so that while I propose to exhibit in my own name as the inventor,* the goods will be under the charge of their assistant, leaving the extra space allotted to me at liberty for other purposes.

SUTTON WORKS, ASTON ROAD, BIRMINGHAM,
July 24th, 1865.

P. L. SIMMONDS, Esq.,
Society of Arts,
John Street, Adelphi.

SIR,—As we did not know through whom we were to send the detailed list of our goods to Oporto Exhibition, we beg to enclose it to you, and shall feel obliged if you will forward it to its proper destination. Whatever the postage on it may be, if you will let us know, we will repay it to you.

We sent our goods to care of Messrs. Ivens & Sons.

We have not heard anything from them, though we have written twice, but we suppose they will be all right.

We remain,
Yours obediently,
J. PARKES & Co.

SUTTON WORKS, ASTON ROAD, BIRMINGHAM,
July 27th, 1865.

Mr. P. L. SIMMONDS,
London.

SIR,—We beg to acknowledge your letter 26th inst. We find, on reference to the regulations Art. 8, that the Committee will open the case of goods we have sent, and as they are spades, shovels and forks,—things not liable to much damage,—we do not think it would be necessary to appoint an agent.

Would you please to apply to the authorities to have our packing-case warehoused to pack the goods in, in case they are not sold?

We remain,
Yours obediently,
J. PARKES & Co.

We think we omitted in our former letter to say that the case of tools, addressed to the Committee of Oporto Exhibition was 5 ft. long, 3 ft. 10 inches wide, and 1 ft. 3 inches deep, and that the weight was 4 cwt.

EXETER, *May 4th*, 1865.

P. L. SIMMONDS, Esq.

SIR,—I enclose demand for space in the Oporto Exhibition. The goods will consist of 2 Tables, the stands walnut; the tops composed of plate glass, in walnut frame, fixed to the stands in the common way of loo tables, to turn up. The tops are enamelled in gold and colours, forming a rich, ornamental, useful drawing-room piece of furniture. The whole of the work is enamelled on the under side of the glass; thus giving brilliancy and durability, as it can never be removed.

I should be obliged if you would let me know where to direct it, when to send it off, and how to arrange the payment of carriage to and fro, and if you could give me an approximate estimate of cost.

I should pack the 2 tops in a case, and the 2 stands simply in straw. Of course, if not sold, they would pack them and return to me at the close.

If they are sent to London, I should like you to see them.

Awaiting your reply,

I remain, Sir,
Yours respectfully,
JOHN BRADLEY.

———

EXETER, *August 11th*, 1865.

P. L. SIMMONDS, Esq.

SIR,—I have this day forwarded by the B. & E.

Railway, to Messrs. Chiffens, the 2 Tables ; the 2 tops
are in a box, and the 2 stands are in one package.
The value of each is £8. Should they not sell, I hope
they will be carefully returned at the close of the Exhibition.

I hope to stand a chance for the medals rather than to
sell the tables, although I have marked them low, that
they may be sold rather than have them returned. If
there are any particulars you may require, I will at any
time communicate them to you.

I thank you for the trouble you have taken, and
hoping to be successful,

I remain, Sir,
Yours respectfully,
JOHN BRADLEY.

BRADFORD, YORKS, 23rd *June*, 1865.

P. L. SIMMONDS, Esq.,
           London, W.C.

DEAR SIR,—We enclose form of request for space in
Portuguese Exhibition, from which you will see we want
10 feet long × 6 feet broad × 9 feet high, and we
should very much like a view all round for the glass
case.

We send you two letters from parties proffering assistance. Will you kindly say whether you know anything

of either of them, and which is the likeliest party?
Please return their letters at the same time.

We are, dear Sir,
Yours truly,
JOSEPH CRAVEN & COMPANY (LIMITED),
Per N. BURNETT.

———

BRADFORD, YORKS, 18th Aug., 1865.

P. L. SIMMONDS, Esq.,
    London, W.C.

DEAR SIR,—Having had no reply to our letter of 23rd
inst., will you please say whether the space applied for
has been granted us? Would you also say whether we
can get a case for the display of the goods made in Portugal for a reasonable sum, or if we shall require to send
one from this country?

We have had so much trouble and disappointment in
connection with the Dublin Exhibition, that were it not
for our desire to carry out the project and give what im-
petus we can to the particular class of manufactures in
colonial wool, we should almost hesitate to face a Foreign
Exhibition.

The favour of your early reply will oblige,

Dear Sir,
Yours obediently,
JOSEPH CRAVEN & Co. (LIMITED),
Per N. BURNETT.

BENTHALL WORKS, BROSELEY, SALOP,

13*th May*, 1865.

SIR,—May we ask the favour of your supplying us with all necessary information regarding the Portuguese International Exhibition, as we are thinking of sending a few Specimen Frames of our Encaustic Tiles in Geometrical Mosaic, for which we shall require some wall-space ?

Will you also kindly inform us whether there will be any organization at Oporto for taking charge of *and fixing* English productions, as we shall not exhibit if it is necessary to send any one out.   In any case, all we shall do will be to send half a dozen square frames, which almost any one on the spot could fix against the wall.

We are, Sir,
Your obedient Servants,
MAW & Co.

P. L. SIMMONDS, Esq.,
Society of Arts,
Adelphi, London.

———

BENTHALL WORKS, BROSELEY, SALOP,

August 5th, 1865.

P. L. SIMMONDS, Esq.

SIR,—We have kept no memorandum of the *Class* and section under which our Specimens were to appear.

We shall therefore be obliged if you will refer to the

application for space, and let us know, as the particulars will be wanted for the addresses of packages, which are nearly ready to send off.

We remain, Sir,

Yours obediently,

MAW & Co.

SHEFFIELD, *July*, 1866.

DEAR SIR,—I sent to the Portuguese Exhibition some cutlery and tools, the freight and charges of which I duly paid, but it was particularly understood with you that no agency charges were to be incurred, and that the committee would open the cases and place the goods. I have now had a bill rendered of £8. 10s. for agency and commission, which I certainly shall not pay, especially as I have not yet received my goods back. The freight home and any incidental packing charges I am, of course, willing to pay. But as I learn that the Portuguese Exhibition has been financially and commercially a failure, it is quite enough to be saddled with the outward and homeward freights to Oporto, without any honorary or business results from our exhibits.

Yours truly,

BURNS & Co.

P. L. SIMMONDS, Esq.

TRADE CIRCULARS AND NOTICES, &c.

Paris, 13, Rue de la Michodière,

May 31st, 1863.

Sir,—I take the liberty of informing you that I have returned to Paris, and beg to send you my present address, as above.

Permit me to add that I have extended my connections abroad, and that I have well-established agencies for Patent and general business in Brussels, the Hague, Vienna, Berlin, Munich, Turin, Washington, New York, Singapore, Hong-Kong, &c.

Your obedient Servant,

G. W. Yapp.

(Announcing formation of a Limited Company.)

Francis Morton & Company (Limited).

Patent Fencing, Galvanizing & Corrugated Iron Works,

Liverpool, 1st *July*, 1864.

Gentlemen,—On behalf of the Directors of "Francis Morton & Company, Limited," I beg leave to advise you, that from the above date, viz. the 1st July, 1864, the business hitherto carried on in the name of Francis Morton & Co. will be continued under the style of

"Francis Morton & Company, Limited," the family of the late Francis Morton, Esq., taking a large interest in the new concern, and Mr. Francis Morton, his son, being one of the Directors.

Among several friends who have also taken a large interest therein, I have the pleasure to name Peter Rylands, Esq., of Bewsey House, Warrington, a member of the well-known firm of "Rylands Brothers," wire-drawers, Warrington, and he has become one of the Directors of the Company.

The Directors have concluded arrangements to continue the business under the Resident Management and Staff of the late firm.

Having now entered into the full occupation of their extensive new works in Naylor Street, Liverpool, the Directors are prepared to execute all orders entrusted to them with the utmost despatch, and on specially advantageous terms.

While thanking you, as one of the numerous friends of the late firm, for your valued support, I beg leave to ask for a continuance of your confidence in the New Company, and to assure you that all future orders and contracts will be executed with the same care and promptitude as heretofore.

I am, Gentlemen,
Yours very obediently,
W. LLEWELLEN DAVIES,
General Manager.

96, STRAND, LONDON, W.C.,

15*th February*, 1862.

DEAR SIR,—Having become co-proprietor of the Manufactory of Perfumery Materials carried on for many years by my late father, Mr. H. Rimmel, I am now in a position to offer you French Pommades, Oils, and Essences of a superior quality, in original packages, at very moderate prices. You know that in making up greases for the hair, you can produce by means of French Pommades and Oils, a beautiful and delicate flavour unobtainable with Essential Oils, whilst at the same time they make those preparations keep much longer. They have not been much used hitherto, owing to their being very expensive ; but you will see by the quotations at foot that I have entirely removed that objection, as the present price will not exceed that of ordinary grease scented with Essential Oils, although the flavour is much finer. I trust, therefore, that you will avail yourself of this advantage, and I am confident that a single trial will convince you of the great improvement it will effect in your preparations.

I remain, dear Sir,

Yours very truly,

E. RIMMEL.

(Dissolution of Partnership.)

NOTICE

Is hereby given that Mr. W. P. Lyons retires this

day, by mutual consent, from the firm of H. Baldwin & Co.

H. A. BALLARD,	II. BALDWIN & Co.
W. P. LYONS,	
H. J. ADAIR.	

YOKOHAMA, *March 20th*, 1866.

With reference to the above, the firm of H. Baldwin & Co. will be continued as heretofore by the undersigned, who will settle all debts of the firm.

H. A. BALLARD.

H. J. ADAIR.

YOKOHAMA, *March 20th*, 1866.

NOTICE.

The interest and responsibility of Mr. John Roberts, jun., in the firm of Jelovitz & Roberts, will cease on the 31st inst., before which time it is requested that all claims against the above firm may be sent in for adjustment, and that all parties indebted to the said firm will settle their accounts before that time.

With reference to the above, the business will be carried on under the style and firm of Jelovitz & Co., from the 1st of April, 1866.

YOKOHAMA, *March 16th*, 1866.

NOTICE.

The partnership hitherto existing between Dominique Rémi de Montigny & Edouard Schmidt, under the style or firm of Rémi, Schmidt, & Co., and carrying on the business of General Merchants at Shaughai, Yokohama, Bangkok, and London, has been this day dissolved by mutual consent.

REMI DE MONTIGNY.
E. SCHMIDT.

SHANGHAI, 1st *March*, 1866.

In consequence of the dissolution of partnership announced above, the undersigned gives notice that he has taken over the interest and responsibility of the late firm of Rémi, Schmidt, & Co., in Shanghai, Bangkok, and London.

M. Edouard Bonneville is authorized to sign his name per procuration.

RÉMI DE MONTIGNY.

SHANGHAI, 1st *March*, 1866.

With reference to the above, the undersigned gives notice that the business hitherto carried on at Yokohama by the late firm of Rémi, Schmidt, & Co., will in future be conducted by him, and that the interest and responsibility of M. Rémi de Montigny in the same has ceased from this day.

Mr. Adrian Devegn is authorized to sign his name per procuration.

E. SCHMIDT

SHANGHAI, 1st *March*, 1866.

NOTICE

Is hereby given, that the co-partnership which has for some time subsisted between M. G. Mackertoom and

Carr Lucas, under the firm and style of Mackertoom & Co., has been dissolved by mutual consent. The undersigned, assuming the responsibilities of the said firm, will in future conduct the business on his own account, under the style of Carr Lucas & Co.

CARR LUCAS.

CANTON, 31*st July*, 1865.

NOTICE

Is hereby given, that the partnership lately subsisting, between Mackertoom Galoost Mackertoom and Carr Lucas, heretofore carrying on business under the firm of Mackertoom & Co., at Canton, was on the 20th day of March, 1865, dissolved by mutual consent. All debts due to the said late co-partnership firm are to be received by the said Carr Lucas, and all persons to whom the said partnership stands indebted are requested to send in their respective accounts for liquidation to the said Carr Lucas, who has assumed the responsibilities of the said late firm, and fully discharged the said Mackertoom Galoost Mackertoom from all liabilities in respect thereto.

M. G. MACKERTOOM.

SINGAPORE, 20*th August*, 1865.

70, CANNON STREET WEST, LONDON, E.C.,
15*th May*, 1866.

NOTICE

Is hereby given, that the partnership heretofore subsisting between us, the undersigned David Wilson, John Randon Worcester, Alexander Calder, and Edmond Collinet, carrying on business at No. 70, Cannon Street West, in the City of London, as East-India Merchants, has been this day dissolved by mutual consent as to the said John Randon Worcester, and the business will in future be carried on by the remaining partners, under the style or firm of "Wilson, Calder, & Co."

Dated this 15th day of May, 1866.

DAVID WILSON.

J. R. WORCESTER.

ALEX. CALDER.

EDMOND COLLINET.

70, CANNON STREET WEST, LONDON,

16th May, 1866.

Having reference to the above notice, we beg to request your attention to the annexed signatures of the several partners of our firm.

WILSON, CALDER, & Co.

Mr. WILSON will sign *Wilson, Calder, & Co.*

Mr. CALDER   ,,   *Wilson, Calder, & Co.*

Mr. COLLINET   ,,   *Wilson, Calder, & Co.*

PENANG, *March 1st*, 1866.

DEAR SIR,—We beg to inform you that Mr. Ferd. H. Friederichs has been admitted a partner in our firm, and respectfully request your attention to his signature at foot.

We remain,

Dear Sir,

Your obedient Servants,

FRIEDERICHS & Co.

Mr. FERD. H. FRIEDERICHS will sign *Friederichs & Co.*

CARRIAGE MANUFACTORY,

28, HAYMARKET, LONDON, W.

GENTLEMEN,—We beg to bring under your notice our Stock of Light, Medium, as well as Full-sized Family Carriages, all of which have been constructed with the utmost care as regards design, workmanship, and materials; they are not only suitable for this country, but, from the thoroughly seasoned timber and materials invariably used, can be confidently recommended for extreme climates, whether hot or cold.

We are in a position to execute orders for handsome Court Carriages in the most artistic and efficient manner, having for many years had great experience in furnishing such carriages to the Queen and Royal Family of England, as well as to several Foreign Courts, and a large number of the English nobility.

Inviting an inspection of our Carriages (which include almost every variety made), when you require any for exportation, and assuring you that we should endeavour to turn out such as would not only satisfy you, and do credit to our manufacture, but secure a continuance of your orders to our house,

We are, Gentlemen,

Your very obedient Servants,

HOOPER & Co.

NOTICES OF SUSPENSION.

SIR,—In consequence of very heavy losses and the present position of financial affairs, we find ourselves unable to continue carrying on our business without making such sacrifices as might imperil our ability to meet all our liabilities in full. We have, therefore, after consultation with our friends, decided on suspending payment, feeling that such a course is the most honourable, and will prove the most beneficial for our creditors.

We have requested Messrs. Coleman, Turquand, Youngs, & Co., to prepare a statement of our affairs without delay, and to convene a meeting, when we hope to submit such proposals for liquidation as will be found acceptable. In the mean time, craving your kind forbearance,

> We remain, Sir,
> Your obedient Servants,
> H. J. ENDERBY & SONS.

MOORGATE STREET, LONDON, *May* 30.

LIVERPOOL, *May* 24, 1866.

We regret to inform you that in consequence of the very serious depreciation in the value of cotton, and the monetary panic prevailing in Bombay, we have been compelled to suspend our payments.

We shall place our books in the hands of Messrs. Harmood, Banner, & Son, who will without delay prepare a statement of our affairs, which shall be submitted to you at an early date.

Meantime soliciting your forbearance,

> We remain,
> Yours faithfully,
> MACCULLOCH, JOHN, & Co.

CIRCULAR TO CREDITORS.

FLEET STREET,

May 16, 1866.

SIR,—We are most happy to inform you that arrangements are in progress with the London Joint-stock Bank by which it is intended that the business heretofore carried on by us will forthwith be conducted as a branch of that establishment at our present offices. With a view to the convenience of the creditors, and to obviate the consequences of delay in realizing the assets, a sum equal to 10*s.* in the pound will, with the assent of the creditors, be advanced by the bank and placed to their credit in account, the bank receiving the dividends payable on the respective claims so far as may be requisite for the liquidation of such advance, and the surplus arising from our estate to be paid to the creditors when realized.

Upon this arrangement being carried out, our Mr. James A. Ballard will be charged with the management of the new branch, and we trust that you will favour the London Joint-stock Bank with your confidence and support.

We are,

Your obedient Servants,

BALLARD, HOSKINS, & Co.

P.S.—It is hoped the new business will be opened on Monday, the 21st instant, when the creditors are requested to call at our offices and make the requisite arrangements.

F. W. COSENS' MONTHLY WINE CIRCULAR.

May 19, 1862.

Viâ Suez.

SIR,—During the period that has elapsed since the departure of the April mail, business in all descriptions of Wines and Spirits has been limited to the demand for immediate consumption ; the trade being evidently averse to stock, so long as they can secure sufficient for their present requirements at moderate prices.

The liberal margin secured at the half-crown rate of duty, prevents annoyance and delay, and practically renders check testings on the part of the merchant unnecessary.   The two rates of one shilling and two and sixpence seem to work well, although of the 2,391,271 gallons of Wine cleared for home consumption, for the three months ending 31st March last, 173,463 gallons only were passed at a shilling duty, against 355,261 for the same period of 1861.

The telegrams from Cognac respecting the frost were in due course confirmed, but since then the weather has taken a more favourable turn, and it is hoped the vintage will prove an average, if not an abundant one, should no further drawbacks arise between the present time and the gathering.

The plan adopted, since the introduction of the new tariff at Melbourne, of quoting Wines at Bonded prices will prove extremely advantageous to the shippers from hence, as it will tend to discourage shipments from small dealers who have been misled by the quotations in the

Prices Current, which included the old duty of 2*s.* per gallon.

WINES.

SHERRY.—The Export from Cadiz continues moderate, and prices of the lower and medium marks are well maintained, while for fine qualities there has been a rise of from £3 to £5 per butt established, caused by the increased demand for England since the reduction of the duty. No direct shipments of Sherry are advised, the *Electra* in January being the last cargo.

PORT.—From Oporto the accounts speak cheerfully of the present appearance of the vineyards, and hopes are entertained that the vintage will prove a good one.

In other Wines nothing of importance calls for special remark.

SPIRITS.

BRANDY.—This market is perfectly inanimate, although the demand for the Home Trade as well as Export continues good.

The following is the result of the Home and Export trade for the quarter ending 31st March of each year :—

1862 .... 505,300 gallons.
1861 .... 476,240 „
1860 .... 406,970 „

RUM.—The price of this Spirit still continues to rule extremely low.

GENEVA & BRITISH SPIRITS.—See quotations.

P.S.—Later advices from France and Portugal report cold weather and severe storms on the Douro.

SILK CIRCULAR.

23, OLD BROAD STREET, LONDON,
1st January, 1864.

The advance in the Bank rate of discount on the 2nd December to 7 per cent., and on the 3rd to 8 per cent., had but little (if any) effect upon the prices of China and Japan Raw Silk ; naturally business was curtailed to some extent by the stringency of the money market, still Importers generally evinced no disposition to give way, and for the few transactions effected, full prices were paid. Since the reduction of the Bank rate to 7 per cent., with symptoms of increasing ease in the money market, buyers show more disposition to do business, but Importers hold their Silk firmer than ever, being encouraged by the strengthening nature of the recent advices from China and Japan.

The deliveries for the month are miserably small, and show how much the consumption of Asiatic Silk has been interfered with, more especially on the Continent, by the abundance and relative cheapness of European Silk.

The China Mail steamer having run ashore in the Red Sea, we are unable to give our usual statistics from Shanghai ; the telegram announces but small settlements for the fortnight (about 1,500 bales), with a further advance in prices. Unsold stock on the market was said to be 11,500 bales.

In Bengal Silk we have no alteration.

In Italian Silk there has been a fair business, without any improvement in prices : the cheapness of European as compared with Asiatic Silk is more apparent than ever.

The Silk Trade for the past year presents no satisfactory feature; consumption, as compared with 1862, has fallen off materially, and although our importations from China have been unusually small, the deficiency has to a great extent been supplied from Japan, and we close the year with an increased and not a diminished stock. The fluctuations in prices during the year have been unimportant. In January and February we had active business with some trifling advance; during March, April, May, and June, the market was quiet, and prices receded 1s. 6d. to 2s. per lb.; towards the latter end of July an improved demand sprung up, which lasted only for a short time: August was, on the whole, a quiet month, and prices experienced a further trifling reduction; making this the lowest moment of the year. In September we had extensive business, resulting in a recovery in price of 1s. to 1s. 6d. per lb., on both China and Japan Silk; but in October, operations were again checked by the extreme pretensions of Importers, and the market has since remained quiet, though prices generally have been well maintained.

WAITHMAN, JACOMB, & HOGG.

TALLOW TRADE CIRCULAR.

LONDON, *May 14th*, 1866.

During the past week this market has been unsteady, prices having fluctuated to the extent of 1s. per cwt. in nearly all positions, alternating from a state of great firmness to one of extreme flatness, as apprehensions of war in Germany and the effects of the existing panic preponderated. The depreciation, however, has not yet extended to a very serious fall, although the circumstances which have occurred in the last few days, both political and financial, distinctly indicate much lower quotations than those now current. *On dit*, that if Prussia attack Austria, Russia will side with the latter; and if this statement be correct, which is most probable, it offers a guarantee that no impediment will present itself in the ensuing months to the usual and regular influx of tallow from Russia.

The most important event, however, is the suspension of the great discount house, the effects of which cannot yet be nearly known or felt. The enormous amount of overtrading in the last twelve months, which has been fostered, and even encouraged, by the facilities afforded by financial companies to speculators and others, whose operations, in a majority of instances, have been of a rash and hazardous character, will probably lead to a series of disasters, which, although they may be individually of small importance when compared with the two most prominent events of last week, yet in the aggregate will probably amount to a very much larger sum, with considerably worse prospects of a satisfactory liquidation.

It is well known that of late years many parties have combined together to monopolize enormous quantities of goods, &c., which, when purchased, have been immediately hypothecated for about 80 per cent. of their value. The difference between the cost price and the loans thus obtained has been raised at discount offices, the sum required for this purpose on so enormous an amount of business being more than could by any other means be raised. The shutting up of the principal source of these supplies has already had a material effect on the quotations, especially those for goods in which speculators generally deal, and which must, under these circumstances, eventually suffer a very considerable depreciation in value.

At sales on Friday last, 561 casks sorts were offered, and only 4 casks fine. Australian beef sold at 46s.

The delivery last week was 1,025 casks against 1,163 last year.

The arrivals in the same period were 338 casks from Australia against 115 in 1865

The market to-day has been very flat, and closes quiet at 45s. to 45s. 6d. spot, 45s. to 45s. 3d. June, and 47s. to 47s. 3d. October to December.

Petroleum 2s. to 2s. 2½d. per gallon.

J. E. TIBBS & SON.

ANNUAL TEA CIRCULAR.

LONDON, January 7th, 1865.

We beg to hand our Annual Report of the Tea Market for the year ending 31st December, 1864 :

The commercial retrospect of the past year is chiefly remarkable for greater fluctuations in the Money market, and a higher rate of discount, than has existed for many years, producing serious disturbance to commercial operations, great depression in many articles of produce, low prices, heavy losses to Importers, and a considerable number of failures. The strain on the energies and resources of the trading community was most intense, and the general soundness of the Commerce of the country was seen in the way in which the pressure was borne. There can be no doubt that we have experienced one of the most trying crises in the commercial history of this country, a much longer continuance of which would have paralyzed enterprise to a great extent, and added largely to the list of failures. In this respect the new year opens with considerable relief. We may hope that the worst is past, and though money may not be much cheaper, we may reasonably anticipate that with the caution which the recent crisis has induced, the operations of the coming year will be of a more profitable and satisfactory character.

An alteration in the Bank rate occurred no less than fifteen times during the year; the highest point reached was 9, and the lowest 6 per cent. The average for the year was from 7 to $7\frac{1}{2}$ per cent., whilst in 1863 the average was about $4\frac{1}{2}$.

Although foreign loans, and the demand for money for India and other Cotton-growing countries, will continue to draw upon our resources, from these will accrue in the long run profitable returns. We trust that one cause of the monetary derangement has received a check; we refer to the reckless financial schemes and speculations which at the commencement of last year engrossed public attention; the legitimate trader was seriously crippled, ordinary facilities withdrawn, and the forced sales of many

articles of produce throughout the year, and the heavy
losses to all concerned, were the penalties paid by the
commercial classes for the encouragement given to these
projects.

The review of the Tea Market shows this article of
consumption to have participated in the general depression. With a few occasional fluctuations, the result of
the year's business has been most unsatisfactory. Stocks
were heavy, Imports excessive, and prices paid in China
much higher than our ruling market rates. Arrivals
were necessarily forced for immediate sale, and entailed
heavy losses, the trade found stock accumulating and
gradually depreciating in value, every sale making previous purchases dear; the close of the year showing a
considerable fall in the prices of most kinds, excepting
the fine descriptions, which have generally maintained
their value, proving that the consumption since the reduction of the duty has been greatly on the better
qualities.

The Deliveries have continued on a satisfactory scale.
For Home Consumption, as will be seen by the annexed
statement, we have an increase of 3,000,000 lb. The
Export trade also shows an increase on the large deliveries for that purpose in 1863. The Imports have been
excessive, nor can our market be expected to recover to
a healthy condition until the shipments from China, and
the prices there paid, are regulated with some regard to
the requirements of the home market.

*Import, Delivery, and Stock of Tea in the United King-
dom for the Year ending* 31*st December*, 1864.

	1864.		1863.		
Import......	123,500,000	against	136,500,000	Decr.	13,000,000 lb.
Delivery	116,500,000	,,	112,750,000	Incr.	3,750,000 ,,
Home Consumption	88,500,000	,,	85,500,000	,,	3,000,000 ,,
Export......	28,000,000	,,	27,250,000	,,	750,000 ,,
Stock	97,000,000	,,	92,000,000	,,	5,000,000 ,,

In January the Tea Market was quiet but holders were
firm, but arrivals being large, the trade, with the prospect
of ample supplies, acted very cautiously. In February
there was an active demand, especially for good and fine
Tea, at rather improved rates. In March there was considerable pressure from recent heavy arrivals, and forced
sales, both by public and private contract, caused a decline
on most descriptions, medium qualities being most affected.
Good common was rather wanted for Export. In May
the advance of the Bank rate to 9 per cent. checked business, but in June advices from China being considered
somewhat favourable, Importers were firm, and the trade
bought freely; some speculative purchases were also
made. In July the Bank rate was reduced to 6 per
cent., but the Tea Market had relapsed into inactivity,
speculation had ceased; Importers, however, were not
inclined to give way. In August the Money market had
become very uneasy, and rapid changes in the rate of discount were made from 6 to 8 per cent.; though Importers
still were firm, a large quantity of second-hand Tea was
forced for sale, and prices declined in some cases considerably. A small parcel of new season's Congou of the *new
make* arrived by the French Overland route, and sold at

3s. 1d. to 3s. 6d. for finest, and 2s. 2d. to 2s. 3d. for the inferior. In September the chief feature was the arrival per Overland route of four chops Moning, and about the same quantity of Kysows. Very high rates were demanded, a few Monings were moved at 3s. to 3s. 1d.; these prices, however, could not be maintained, and several chops were taken for export at from 2s. 8d. to 2s. 10d. Kysows sold slowly at 2s. 7d. to 2s. 11d. In October, advices from China showed heavy shipments, and the greatest gloom and uneasiness existing on the money market. Importers were anxious to realize, the market had to bear the pressure of large quantities forced for unreserved sale, and prices declined considerably in old season's Tea. New Monings sold slowly, but fine Kysows were in demand, and prices rather improved. The arrival of twenty-three vessels, the cargoes of which were at once placed on the market, at a time when daily failures created the greatest uneasiness in commercial circles, caused most irregular sales, the question not being so much actual value as a determination to realize at the best obtainable price. This state of things continued till nearly the close of the year. The favourable change in the Money market, the Bank rate being reduced to 6 per cent. on the 15th December, put holders in better spirits, and the new year was looked forward to in expectation of an improved business.

W. E. FRANKS & SONS.

TEA CIRCULAR FOR MAY, 1866.

We beg to tender to our numerous customers our acknowledgments and thanks.

The season at which the Chancellor of the Exchequer makes his financial arrangements for the year, seems a fitting one for offering any information and observations upon the subject of our trade.

Whether looked at from a commercial or social point of view, the growing importance of the Tea Trade is remarkable ; on the one hand, we have a vastly increased rate of gross consumption, and a rate per head never before attained in this country, and the revenue derived from it in a rapidly recovering state ; on the other, it is a fair matter for congratulation that the increase in the use of this article by the great bulk of the population is attended with social and domestic advantages.

According to the Budget of Monday last, there will be no further disturbance in the Tea Duty for the next twelve months.

With regard to the price and supply, the growth of Tea in our British Indian possessions increases to a great extent, and the qualities of the Finest Assams are beginning to be highly appreciated from the great strength they possess.

In China, the varying fortunes of war in the Tea-growing districts cause corresponding fluctuations in the first price of the article ; still, notwithstanding an unprecedented demand, there is nothing to cause any considerable advance during the next few months.

We may report favourably of the Bonded Stock of Teas. We are holders of some very fine parcels of Black as well as Green Teas, qualities equalling any former period.

For our Price List we refer as below, only in conclusion calling particular attention to the fact that we are sending out Caddies, about 12 lb. each, of all our finest Black Teas, at a reduction of 2d. per lb. upon our regular prices.

T. & A. WRIGHT.

STEAM-SHIPPING CIRCULAR.

Some improvement in steam-shipping has taken place within the past month, but it is only partially sustained, and there is not at this moment any prospect of its continuance. A few sales have been effected of new steamers at fair prices, but the demand for second-hand has been limited. The chartering has been inactive ; low rates for good useful steamers on time still prevail, with little demand.

Freights to and from the Baltic have experienced no improvement, and rates remain dull. Moderate inquiries have taken place, principally for coals, to the Mediterranean. Homeward cargoes are, however, scarce.

No demand has yet taken place for fruit cargoes, which usually occurs at this period.

ALFRED BRETT & Co.

MAURITIUS SUGAR MARKET.

Oct. 6, 1864.

The weather having recently proved more favourable for the manufacture of Sugar, it is now being carried on with much activity on all the estates, and although the crop is unusually late, only 11,500 tons having been shipped up to the 30th ult., against 21,000 tons at the same date last year, we believe that our product this season will aggregate from 110,000 to 120,000 tons.

The somewhat unsatisfactory advices of the London Sugar Market received by last packet caused a decline in the value of grey refining sugar of about 10 cents per 100 lb. ; but at this reduction in price there is now a good demand for Europe.

Our exports to the Australian colonies since this season opened, say from 1st of August to the 30th ult., have been on a very moderate scale, aggregating only 1,700 tons, while, during the corresponding period last season, they were 6,359 tons. The shipments during this month will, however, be unusually heavy.

Taking freight to the United Kingdom at 60*s.* per ton, and exchange at $4\frac{3}{4}$ per cent. discount, we estimate the cost of a good grey refining sugar at about 27*s.* per cwt. free on board.

Taking freight to the Australian colonies at 50*s.*, and exchange at 6 per cent. discount, we estimate the cost of a fine first counter yellow grocery sugar at 30*s.* 6*d.* per cwt. free on board.

The following is a comparative statement showing the

exports of Sugar as compared with the two preceding seasons, &c.

IRELAND, FRASER, & Co.

REPORT ON THE HARDWARE AND METAL TRADES.

In connection with the iron and machine trades of Leeds, we may note that there is fair employment for the workmen in the various forges in and about the town, but business has not yet so fully developed itself as it was expected might have been the case after the termination of the American war.

The ironfounding business is in a very animated state, and even the newly started firms enjoy a large share of trade.

At Sheffield the cutlery branches have so much improved of late that the workmen are generally agitating for advanced wages. The saw trade is more active than it has been for a considerable time past, owing chiefly to the improved trade with America ; all the good workmen are well employed, and the trades' union funds, which had for some time been heavily drawn upon by the unemployed, are being replenished. The edge and general tool trades are also active. The silver-plating and Britannia metal branches are languid, and the steel trade continues dull in most branches.

There is a good home demand for rod and bar steel for trade purposes, and the railway orders for the home and foreign markets are good ; but the American and general foreign steel trade continues small.

METAL TRADE CIRCULAR.

The unsettled state of the money market, coupled with the uncertainty of Continental politics, continues to press heavily on all kinds of metals. Consumers and shippers only buy for their most pressing wants, and even the comparative low prices now ruling do not attract the attention of speculators.

IRON.—We cannot report any change in the position of Welsh and Staffordshire ; the demand is very slack, and for good specifications makers are willing to make concession.   Scotch pig now rules at 50s. 9d. cash.

COPPER.—We have to report a much better market ; a large business doing in English raw and manufactured at fixed prices.   The smelters are now refusing orders. Foreign is also in better demand ; 87l. to 88l. paid for both Burra and Wallaroo, and further buyers ; 81l. for Chili bars and 86l. 10s. for Chili ingots.

TIN.—Quite neglected.   A few small lots of Straits have changed hands from 75l. to 76l., according to quality and shape.   Banca nominally 78l.   English obtainable under official quotations.   The Dutch market is dull at 44½fl.

TIN PLATES.—Hardly anything doing ; prices tending downwards.

LEAD.—Without change.

SPELTER.—Very little business done.   We quote spot from 20l. 10s. to 20l. 15s. ; 21l. for July and August. Special marks in outports have been done at 20l. 17s. 6d.

VON DADELSON & NORTH.

LONDON WOOL CIRCULAR.

LONDON, *Sept. 4th*, 1865.

During the present series of our London Wool Sales, which commenced on the 17th ult., the following have been brought forward ; this day's catalogue included—

17,848	Bales	Sydney.
11,376	„	Port Phillip.
6,414	„	Van Diemen's Land.
3,999	„	Adelaide.
12,932	„	New Zealand.
14,633	„	Cape.
559	„	Sundries.

67,761 Bales.

The competition has been fair, but the foreign buyers have as yet hardly taken their usual proportion.

As compared with the close of the last series, prices for all good Australian and Cape Wools are a shade in favour of the sellers, whilst, on the other hand, defective descriptions are rather easier. Lamb's Wool of all sorts is scarce, and being likewise in good demand, realizes about $\frac{1}{2}d.$ @ $1\frac{1}{2}d.$ per lb. more than in May.

In Donskoi Wool a large business has been done in shipments to arrive, at prices equal to about $11d.$ @ $13\frac{1}{2}d.$ per lb. delivered here,—usual conditions.

Owing to the small stocks consequent upon the large consumption, and also to the decreased export this season, the value of this article is improving.

The following refers to West Coast Wools in Liverpool :—

	Lima & Chili. Bales.	Peruvian. Ballots.
Stock 1st August..................	248	11,872
Imported during August...........	112	719
	360	12,591
Sales in August..................	161	3,508
Stock 1st September..............	199	9,083
Shipped and on passage, as far as advices received.................	416	664

The Board of Trade returns for the seven months ending 31st July show :—

	1864. lb.	1865 lb.
Total Import Sheep & Lambs' Wool..	101,514,291	113,848,148
„ „ Alpaca & Llama ditto..	1,241,192	1,323,862
„ Export Sheep & Lambs' Wool, (Foreign and Colonial)	26,979,025	49,734,290
„ „ British „ „ ..	5,899,633	5,018,710
„ „ Alpaca & Llama ditto ..	2,488	615

HELMUTH SCHWARTZE,

Wool Broker.

3, MOORGATE-STREET BUILDINGS, E.C.

LONDON WOOL CIRCULAR.

LONDON, 14*th May*, 1866.

The second series of this year's London Public Sales of Colonial Wool commenced on the 10th inst., and up to date the catalogues have comprised :—

1,991	Bales	Sydney.
10,109	„	Port Phillip.
895	„	Van Diemen's Land.
1,568	„	Adelaide.
656	„	New Zealand.
10	„	Swan River.
2,794	„	Cape.
244	„	Sundries.

18,267 Bales.

The total arrivals in time consist of :—

25,833	Bales	Sydney.
79,673	„	{ Port Phillip.
20,999	„	Adelaide.
1,961	„	Swan River.
5,704	„	Van Diemen's Land.
16,935	„	New Zealand.
13,428	„	Cape, Eastern Province.
2,294	„	„ Western „

166,827 Bales.

The attendance of buyers from the home districts and from France is very fair, but as yet Germany and Belgium are but poorly represented.

The large quantity to be catalogued, added to the existing political and financial crisis, has had the natural effect of lowering prices, which must be quoted, as compared with the closing rates of last March sales, 1½d. @ 2½d. per lb. lower for both Australians and Capes.

Stocks in the hands of manufacturers and dealers being much reduced, and orders in possession of the former large, whilst their stores of manufactured goods are small, it is generally thought that the prices now ruling will be firmly maintained throughout the series, notwithstanding the very adverse circumstances already mentioned, and it is expected that consumers will take advantage of the present depressed state of the market to lay in stocks.

I quote now—

			s.	d.	s.	d.	
Good Australian clothing	...	1	9½	@ 2	6	per lb.
„	„	combing	...	1	10	„ 2	6	„
„	„	greasy	......	1	1	„ 1	5½	„
„	Cape		......	1	7	„ 1	11	„
,	„	medium	...	1	4½	„ 1	6½	„
„	„	greasy	......	0	9	„ 0	10	„

Colonial Wool Sales will close on the 26th June instead of 20th, as originally arranged.

At Liverpool the Public Sales of East-India Wool, which commenced on the 3rd inst., closed on the 10th, the catalogues having comprised 12,615 bales.

The attendance of buyers was good, but the selection of Wools offered poor, the greater part being inferior badly washed Wools. As compared with last Sales closing rates, fine Wools fetched very full prices, perhaps rather higher. Good qualities were without change, but lower descriptions met with an average reduction of 1*d*. per lb. 1,400 bales Persian were advertised, but were not offered, being in the meanwhile sold on the Continent.

The following Sundry Wools will be offered at Liverpool from the 15th to the 17th inst. :—

2,920	Bales	Turkey.
870	„	Cordova and Monte Video.
630	„	Buenos Ayres and E. Rios.
900	„	Lima and Chili.
1,870	„	Russian.
800	„	Egyptian.
1,560	„	Portuguese.
380	„	Mogadore.
680	„	Sundries.
1,500	„	Peruvian.

12,110 Bales.

The Bank of England raised the rate of discount on the 8th inst. from 7 to 8 per cent. ; on the 11th from 8 to 9 per cent. ; and on the 12th from 9 to 10 per cent.

HELMUTH SCHWARTZE,
Wool Broker.

3, MOORGATE-STREET BUILDINGS, E.C.

LIVERPOOL WOOL CIRCULAR.

GENTLEMEN,—Our Wool Market during the past month has been very quiet; the financial crisis and great depreciation in the value of Cotton have had the effect of rendering buyers extremely cautious, and of limiting their transactions to the supply of immediate wants. On the other hand, Stocks continue light, and holders are unwilling to make any but very moderate concessions in prices. The position of the trade generally is healthy.

Our second series of public sales for the present year closed last night. East-India Wools were sold from the 3rd to the 9th inst.; the quantity brought forward was 12,008 bales. The attendance of the Home Trade was good throughout, but there was hardly an average muster of Foreign buyers. A large proportion of the Wools offered was very faulty. Many parcels were unwashed, and loaded with sand and dirt, and in not a few cases no attempt appears to have been made to sort qualities or colours. It was almost impossible accurately to estimate the per-centage of waste on these descriptions; they consequently sold with much irregularity, and the result will, no doubt, cause disappointment. It is absolutely necessary that more care should be bestowed on the sorting and cleaning in Bombay, otherwise these Wools will suffer in the estimation of our manufacturers. The fine and good middling classes were scarce, and they sold with great spirit at an advance of $\frac{1}{2}d.$ to $1d.$ per lb. ; extraordinary prices were realized for a few bales of choice White, the best selling at $2s.$ $1\frac{1}{2}d.$ per lb. All clean middle class Wools brought fully January prices. Persian Wools were in demand, but the quality of the parcels offered was only second rate, and hardly suitable for export. In the absence of Foreign competition, prices declined $1\frac{1}{2}d.$ to $2d.$ per lb.

The sales of Miscellaneous Wools were not marked by much animation. In all, 11,801 bales were offered, but only a small proportion was disposed of at prices showing an average decline of $1d.$ to $1\frac{1}{2}d.$ per lb. The demand ran chiefly on Mogadore, unwashed Lima, and low Russian Wools. A few small parcels of Iceland and Oporto Cotts and Lambs were sold at rather easier prices.

We have no change to report in the value of Alpaca ; in the absence of recent transactions, the price remains as last quoted.

ENGLISH AND IRISH.—The market for Home-grown Fleeces is depressed and somewhat lower, with very little business doing at present.

> We are, Gentlemen,
> Your most obedient Servants,
> PERKINS & ROBINSON.

VICTORIA BUILDINGS, HACKINS HEY, LIVERPOOL,
18th May, 1866.

BEET-ROOT SUGAR CIRCULAR.

April, 1866.

A great breadth of beet will be sown this year in France ; and this is not to be wondered at, as, even in less favourable seasons than the last, the cultivation of beet remunerates the farmer far better than that of wheat, or of any other agricultural produce. Contracts for the root have already been made by the manufacturers, at equal to 15s. per ton. The production per statute acre on good land during the late season has been from 20 to 24 tons, and the manufacturer has extracted from the root from 7 to 8 per cent. of sugar. Eighteen new manufactories are now being erected in France, which will bring the number up to 437. The quantity of beet sugar manufactured up to the end of February amounted to 242,000 tons, against 141,000 at the same period last year, and 20,000 to 25,000 tons are still likely to be produced (mostly of the browner sorts), making in all between 260,000 and 270,000 tons. There remained in the entrepôts, on the 1st March, 1866, 63,000 tons, against 39,000 tons last year. The stocks of cane in all the ports were at the same time 33,000 against 34,000 in 1865, and 53,000 in 1864. In the Belgian sugar districts 30,000 tons were produced, making in all, in round numbers, 300,000 tons in the two countries. In 1855-56, 275 manufactories produced only 90,000 tons, but the constant discovery of new appliances and of improved methods enables the manufacturer to extract a larger per-centage, and a superior quality from the root. There has been some activity in beet sugar in the Zollverein during the past month. Parcels of strong low qualities have been purchased for the United Kingdom, and the better medium sorts for the inland refineries. The fine white crystallized sorts have been readily taken by Russia, the only country in Europe which has suffered from a deficient crop. The out-turn of the crop will be a full average, both in the Zollverein, Austria, and her possessions. The consumption, however, might keep better pace with the production, seeing the small quantity these countries consume in comparison with the United Kingdom, in which latter is absorbed per head nearly three times as much as in France, four and a half times as much as in the Zollverein, and sixteen times as much as in Austria. In this latter country the use of sugar last year has diminished from $3\frac{1}{4}$ lb. to $2\frac{3}{4}$ lb. per head. Fourteen new factories have been erected in the Zollverein. It is calculated that not less than 600,000 tons of beet sugar have been produced in Europe this season.

ARNOLD BARUCHSON & Co.

MONTHLY STATEMENT OF E. I. HEMP AND FIBRE MARKET.

27, Leadenhall Street, London, E.C.,

Monday, May 9th, 1864.

Jute.—Notwithstanding the large consumption which is going on in this article, yet the arrivals have been so unusually heavy, and the money market so unfavourable to speculation, that a further considerable decline must be noted in the value of common, ordinary, and middling descriptions. Good and fine sorts, from their comparative scarcity and general demand, although not commanding quite previous rates, have yet been but little affected. The prices both at public auction and by private sale show considerable irregularity, establishing an average decline, compared with last month, of 10*s.* on fine, 30*s.* on medium, and 50*s.* to 60*s.* on very ordinary and low common. For arrival the reported sales reach 5,000 bales, comprising, amongst others, S & Co. C in diamond £25; AS & Co. D & K £27 and £24; public and private sales on the spot reaching about 17,000 bales more. Our market closes dull, rejections £14, very ordinary to common £15 to £18. 10*s.*, middling £20 to £22, fair £22 to £23, good £25 to £27, fine £28 to £29. 10*s.*

Jute Cuttings in very little demand, and sales very

trifling ; 500 bales on spot realized £9. 15s. to £10. 5s. cash.

MANILLA HEMP.—There is little change to notice. Our market has been very quiet, and with the decline which has taken place in Baltic Hemp, there has been but little done. Private sales on spot are 4,550 bales at £34 for good old, up to £36. 10s. for fine Albay. For arrival 500 bales June, July, and August delivery £35. At auction, of 3,200 bales exposed, only 950 bales sold, middling £34 to £35, Quilot £45.

SUNN HEMP.—The better sorts in fair request for export, but ordinary and common sorts neglected. Sales 411 bales, ordinary to common £21 to £24, good fair to good £28. 5s. to £29. 15s.

BOMBAY HEMP declining in value, 84 bales common to middling sold, £24. 5s. to £24. 10s.

KURRACHEE HEMP.—With heavy arrivals, a considerable part of that recently landed being damaged, and the quality generally indifferent, prices have declined £3 to £4 per ton, with only moderate sales. Of 1,240 bales offered, 300 bales sold, common £17. 5s. to £20, good fair £25.

CHINA GRASS has commanded more attention, and several sales have been made to speculators at £40 to £41 for middling ; good and fine £46 to £48. 1,200 bales at auction mostly taken in, a few lots of retted, slight damaged, selling £37. 10s. to £40.

COIR YARN.—Until the present week the supplies brought to sale have been small, and dealers being moderately stocked, our market has been firmer, with ready buyers at 20s. to 40s. advance. The sales to date are, *Cochin*—1,400 bales, common to fair £25 to £28, good fair to good £29. 5s. to £35, fine small £41. 15s. to £48. 15s. ; 66 tons Dolls, common to fair £22. 5s. to £24. 10s. ; *Bombay*—240 bales ordinary £23. 10s., middling £27. 15s. to £28, 5 tons middling Dolls £25 ; *Ceylon*—240 bales ordinary £21, middling to fair £25 to £28, good fair to good £30 to £36. 15s., fine £41. 15s. to £46, extra £50 to £50. 10s., 257 tons Dolls, very ordinary to common £21. 15s. to £22. 10s., middling £23 to £25, good £27 to £31. 10s., fine £34 to £40, fine small £45 to £47. 10s.

Coir Fibre.—A further decline of £2 to £3 has been established on the sales of the past month. The demand at present is moderate, and supplies liberal. Sales are, *Bombay*—450 bales ordinary to common £17. 10s. to £20. 5s. ; 18 bales and 3 tons *Ceylon*—common £22 ; *Cochin*—194 bales, fair £23. 15s. to £24. 15s., fine to superior, £26. 5s. to £28. 15s. ; 200 bundles brush £34.

Coir Junk.—Market barely supplied, prices without change. Sales are 5 tons Cochin at £22. 10s. to £22. 15s.

Coir Rope still in very limited demand, with trifling sales. 1,192 coils *Cochin* 1½ to 2 inch sold £23. 15s. ; 130 coils ordinary Ceylon held £21 to £22.

Charles Spurling,
27, Leadenhall Street.

LIVERPOOL MONTHLY COTTON CIRCULAR.

ADELAIDE BUILDINGS, CHAPEL STREET, LIVERPOOL,

1st March, 1865.

We have again to review a month of extreme depression in the Cotton market and a stagnation of business in the manufacturing districts up to the last few days that has seldom been exceeded. Prices show a decline for the month averaging about 1d. per lb.

Our last report left the market in a very depressed state, with Fair Egyptians at 21d., Dhollerah at 17d., and Bengal at 9d. The ruling influences were vague rumours of approaching negotiations in America, and the pressure of a large and increasing stock. A gust of warlike news, however, produced a temporary spurt. Spinners, attracted by the low prices to which Egyptians had fallen, bought largely for one or two days, and Fair quality advanced to 23d. Surats moved ½d. to 1d. per lb. But the rally was very brief. Manchester failed to respond, the arrivals of Egyptian and other long stapled Cotton continued remarkably large, and the former feeling of depression returned. The advance was almost lost immediately, and for several days extreme stagnation prevailed both in Manchester and here, and prices sank rather beneath the lowest point touched before.

When the market was in this sluggish state, a sudden panic was created by the arrival on the 15th ultimo of extraordinary advices from America. It was announced that President Lincoln and Mr. Seward had held an interview with three Commissioners from the South,.with the object of trying whether a peaceful arrangement was practicable. The news came like a thunder clap upon us ; never since the war commenced had the prospect of a settlement appeared so promising, for it was supposed that the Northern President would not have opened negotiations personally without good reasons for expecting a successful issue. During the single day that this news acted on our market, prices fell 1*d*. to 2*d*. per lb., and fair Egyptians were sold as low as 1 *d*., and middling fair Dhollerah at 12½*d*.

The very next day a later steamer from America brought news of the failure of the peace conference. Neither side was willing to abate anything on the vital question of Southern independence, Lincoln demanding as the first condition the surrender of that claim, and the Southern delegates refusing to consider it. Our market partly recovered the decline, but the improvement was not maintained. The repeated shocks given to confidence had completely unnerved the commercial public, especially in Manchester and the manufacturing districts ; the depression there seemed only to grow more intense from week to week ; buyers of goods and yarns held back, and would only purchase the most trifling quantities ; the large stock of Cotton in Liverpool and London, which kept steadily increasing, attracted universal attention and the opinion grew strong and general that the supply of Cotton was increasing so fast as to justify and necessitate a comparatively moderate scale of prices. A deep-seated uneasiness was also felt in regard to American affairs. Though the negotiations had failed, many persons contended that a compromise was not impossible. The way was paved, it was said, for the future interchange of proposals between the warring powers, and, at all events, the first step was taken in the direction of peace. The state of credit in the manufacturing districts was also seriously canvassed, failures began to take place amongst spinners, and more were expected to follow ; the heavy losses caused by this last decline on all who held stocks, coming on the back of the panic of last October, were telling with alarming effect upon the resources of the trade, weakened as these had been by the three years of very unprofitable business. Besides this, many Spinners had suffered severely by importing Egyptian Cotton, which at present prices shows a loss of 6d. to 7d. per lb.

These various causes produced a degree of discouragement in Manchester, as great as occurred last October, and prices fell even lower than on that occasion, good makes of Indian shirtings being sold at about 1s. 10d. per lb., or 8d. per lb. below the rates ruling at the end of the year. In Liverpool, the general scale of prices sank to the level of the panic day, with the exception of Egyptians, which kept about 19d. per lb.

There has been, however, in the last few days a decided change for the better in all the departments of the Cotton trade. The latest advices from America show conclusively that the recent negotiations were abortive, and have set at rest all hopes or fears of an immediate settlement there. Released from this apprehension, the long suspended demand in Manchester has been let loose on a rather considerable scale, the attention of the public has been called to the extraordinary withholding of orders for goods which for months past has taken place, and the large arrears of business that have consequently to be made up, and this is set off against the heavy stocks of Cotton ; the result being that it is now considered safe to do a moderate amount of business at the present level of prices. Pretty large orders have consequently been given out in Manchester, and as Spinners are entirely bare of Cotton they have been obliged to enter our Market freely, and for two or three days the sales ranged from 10,000 to 15,000 bales, the demand chiefly running upon long-stapled Cotton, which advanced $1d.$ to $1\frac{1}{2}d.$ per lb., while Surats and other short staples only improved about $\frac{1}{2}d.$ per lb. Yesterday, however, a tamer feeling came over the market, and it appears likely that the slight improvement will soon be lost.

The money market throughout the past month has continued easy, with the Bank rate at five per cent., and there does not appear to be much prospect of a change in any way for some time.   •

With regard to the prospects of our market, it may be observed that we have seldom passed through a period of greater disappointment to all engaged in the trade. The cheerful anticipations entertained at the close of last year have been entirely falsified, and the many false starts which this market and that of Manchester have taken, followed by relapses into greater depression than before,

have produced a degree of timidity and irresolution seldom
or never witnessed in the history of the trade.

The two leading causes of depression as already observed
have been the rapid increase of stock, and the repeated
spasms of uneasiness about the state of matters across
the Atlantic.   The former of these has been the most
powerful in its influence, and occupies at present the
largest share of attention.   The stock in Liverpool and
London shows an increase of 407,000 bales upon last
year, being 715,000 bales against 308,000 bales.   This
increase has arisen in a great measure from the rapidity
with which the supplies of long-stapled Cotton have come
forward, the import of American, Brazil and Egyptian
Cotton into Liverpool so far being 184,000 bales against
93,000 bales last year.   The trade on the other hand
have only taken at the rate of 21,000 bales per week
against an average delivery last year of 29,000 bales,
showing that they have abstained from buying to the '
utmost of their power.   Everything has contributed this
year to throw the whole weight of stocks into the ports,
and to give currency to an exaggerated notion of the
magnitude of available supplies.   But when account is
taken of the great decrease in shipments on the way from
the East, and of the complete exhaustion of stocks in the
hands of consumers both here and on the Continent, the
importance of these figures is much reduced.   It is
probable that Lancashire was never more bare of Cotton
or its products than it is at the present time, and the
same is believed to be true of the Continent, so that it is
likely there are 100,000 bales less in the hands of consumers than at this time last year.   Estimating the

China mail at two piculs, the amount of Cotton afloat from India and China is 200,000 bales less than last year, so that the deficiency from those two sources is 300,000 bales, to be set off against 407,000 bales of surplus in the stock, making the real excess of the raw material only 107,000 bales.

Of course it must be remembered that the effect of stocks in the ports upon prices is much greater than when part of the burthen is borne by consumers or represented by floating cargoes, and it seems likely that throughout this year there will be a strong tendency to allow stocks to accumulate in the entrepôts, as spinners both here and abroad are straitened alike in courage and resources, and their policy is likely to be a hand to mouth business. They will only buy when they have orders in hand, and even then they will run the risk of not covering themselves until supplies are absolutely wanted. So long as stocks remain about present figures there will be no fear of any sudden start from speculative operations, and the trade is likely to be restricted to the ordinary interchange between importers and consumers in a far greater degree than has been the case for some years past. It may be observed, too, that the enormous losses sustained by holders of Cotton this year, coming as they do so close upon the crushing disaster of last September and October, have diminished their powers of controlling the market, and less capital is available for upholding the price of Cotton than has been the case for the last three or four years. To this cause must be attributed in part the present willingness of holders to meet the demand in spite of their heavy losses, for they feel that the current of events has gone decidedly against them, and that it is vain to struggle against it any longer.

There remains, however, a great source of strength to the market, in the circumstance that stocks of goods have been allowed to run to a point of exhaustion, perhaps never witnessed since the Cotton trade attained any magnitude. At the mills, in the warehouses of Manchester, in the retail shops, in the entrepôts abroad, and even in the interior of Asiatic countries, there is an unprecedented bareness of stocks; the Cotton trade throughout the world is in a state of suspense, and the effect of peace in America is already in a great measure "discounted." It is certain that the "wear and tear" of goods is going on at a rate much above the present production in Lancashire, and still more above the present outgoings of Cotton from the ports, and with intermediate stocks so nearly extinguished, it is highly probable that the demand for goods in Manchester, and for Cotton in Liverpool, will be much larger as the season advances. Buyers are only waiting for prices to settle to such a point as appears to them safe in view of the large stocks of Cotton, and the chance of peace in America, and when that point is attained (which may be the case already), there will be in all probability a large though gradual resumption of business. The accounts from the Calcutta market in particular are very encouraging, a large margin of profit is shown on current quotations, and already a considerable business is doing for that quarter.

With regard to American affairs, we may observe, that there is no prospect at present of peace through the medium of negotiations. The late abortive attempt showed that the pretensions of the two parties were irreconcilable, and the defiant war meetings since held at Richmond prove that the spirit of the South is not yet broken. It is likely we will hear now of a vigorous resumption of hostilities, and of desperate struggles along the Atlantic seaboard, and especially in South Carolina. It is doubtful, however, if the waning resources of the South can maintain the contest on anything like equal terms, and it is not unlikely we may hear of further disasters to their arms. If this be the case there will be renewed fits of disquietude among those engaged in the Cotton trade, for it will be imagined from time to time that the South is about to succumb. We believe its resources and spirit are still equal to a lengthened prosecution of the contest ; but it is important to observe that the Confederate Congress has refused to sanction the arming and emancipation of the slaves. Those in this country who believed in the ultimate success of the South have relied very much upon the aid that emancipated negroes could render to the cause ; but if it be the case that the South will not, or dare not employ this weapon, there will be much less confidence in its success, and the opinion will become general, that it is only a question of time till its resistance is overpowered. If, however, the Federal forces succeed in gradually occupying the Cotton States, the stores of Cotton will probably be burned as they advance, so that the subjugation of the South (if that should be the issue of the war) might release but a small supply of Cotton ; and as the next planting season will occur in the heat of the campaign, very little ground will be sown. These facts materially diminish the importance of peace in America, in connection with the supply of Cotton to this country.

It may be observed that the consumption this year will run more largely upon long-stapled Cotton than heretofore; it is now relatively cheaper and more abundant than short-stapled, and will be profusely supplied during the spring months. It is not unlikely that the consumption will develope to such an extent as to produce scarcity in the latter part of the year, more especially if the Egyptian crop only turns out equal to the last one, as many houses in Alexandria now advise.

SMITH, EDWARDS & Co.,
Cotton Brokers.

MANCHESTER GOODS CIRCULAR.

MANCHESTER, *March* 1, 1865.

We have again to record a very unsatisfactory state of business during the month just closed, in all departments of our market, and notwithstanding several efforts to rally them, a further considerable decline in the prices of Cotton, of Yarns, and of Goods. The first of these efforts was made on the arrival of the steamer from America, on Saturday the 4th ult., when a smart advance took place in Cotton, and was followed by an advance in the prices of Yarns of 1*d.* to 2*d.* per lb., and in India Shirtings of 6*d.* to 9*d.* per piece. But the effect of the advance in prices was immediately to check buying, and the nominal improvement was very short-lived. During the remainder of the week following after Tuesday, the little demand that had arisen quite subsided, and was succeeded by renewed depression, and by a further decline in prices. During the following week there was quite a panic for one day, in consequence of the news that Mr. Lincoln and Mr. Seward had gone to meet some gentlemen on an official mission from the Southern Confederacy, with a view to endeavouring to bring the war to an end. Cotton immediately declined 2*d.* to 3*d.* per lb., and our market became equally prostrate and utterly stagnant. And although on the following day the news arrived of the failure of the negotiations, and the previous day's decline was partially, it has never since been entirely recovered, in either the Liverpool Cotton Market, or with us in Manchester. Dulness was still the characteristic, and in the absence of demand prices continued to droop until Friday last, when a comparatively active demand sprung up for Cotton, and a pretty large amount of orders were placed in our market. The improvement continued, and was extended on the following day; but by Monday it became quite evident that buyers here were quite indisposed to pay any advance, and that holders of Cotton were wishful to realize. The tone of our market was again further impaired yesterday, and the little improvement gained at the end of last week has again been quite lost, prices having virtually receded to about last week's lowest point. The retrograde movement on this last occasion was principally brought about by the occurrence of a large failure in Bolton of a Spinner, and by the announcement of the suspension cf a leading firm in London engaged in the China trade. Such events naturally lead to rumours and fears of other impending disasters, and greatly militate against the return of confidence, already so repeatedly shaken by the rapid recurrence of peace rumours from America, and unsettled by the rapid accumulation of the stock of Cotton in the ports. Thus speculation is discouraged and checked just at a time when importers of the raw material most want its aid to enable them to dispose of their stocks, and the value of which has so seriously declined. Spinners on their side also have been deterred from buying to nearly the extent of the actual consumption, in consequence of the decline in the prices of Yarns and Goods, and because also they find it their true policy to bring their stock of the raw material to its minimum working point, and to keep it there until they become satisfied that Cotton will cease to accumulate in importers' hands, as it has been doing for some months past week by week. The stocks in Liverpool and London together are estimated at 715,000 bales now, against 308,000 bales at the same time last year. It is not, however, to be supposed that the "trade" can continue to buy so sparingly as they have been doing heretofore since the end of the year, unless there is a very much more extensive closing of mills than has so far taken place, and which we certainly do not anticipate, for it is fair to suppose that as prices fall the consumption of Yarns and Goods will everywhere extend. It is consequently more probable that other mills will be re-opened that have long been closed, than that those now at work should be extensively closed. So that we may look for a larger and more steady demand ere long for Cotton by the "trade." And although the import of Cotton has so far been considerably in excess this year, over the corresponding period of last, the quantities now on the water from India and China are very considerably less, a feature which may be expected to continue, as the advices sent out have been so very discouraging. Whilst a continuance of high prices would have drained India of all the Cotton grown and not absolutely required for home consumption, and would have led to increasing importation from China, the case may be very different from those distant markets, now that prices have fallen so much, and that confidence in the future of the staple is so greatly impaired. But this last remark has more bearing on the more distant than on the immediate future, before which other matters may modify and change our prospects, that have not yet come into play. Meantime, however, business in Cotton, and in all its products, is unusually perplexing and anxious for all concerned therein, and there will, apparently be but little satisfaction in it until something like normal prices are once more gained.

The actual decline in prices within the past month amounts to $1\frac{1}{2}d.$ to $2d.$ per lb. on low qualities of Yarns, and also on India No. 40's ; $2d.$ to $3d.$ per lb. on medium qualities, and $4d.$ to $6d.$ per lb. on the finer kinds ; 7-8ths Printers have declined $3d.$ to $1s.$ per piece ; Madapollams, $3d.$ to $9d.$; 9-8ths Printers, $3d.$ to $1s.$; India Shirtings, $6d.$ to $1s.$ per piece ; low Reed Jacconets, $6d.$ to $9d.$, and Medium qualities, $4\frac{1}{2}d.$ to $6d.$ per piece ; 39 in. Mulls, $3d.$, and 45 in. Green-end, about $6d.$ per piece ; T Cloths, $9d.$, and Long-cloths, $6d.$ to $1s.$ per piece, and Domestics are $\frac{1}{8}d.$ to $\frac{1}{4}d.$ per yard lower.

GEORGE FRASER, SON, & Co.

BUSINESS FORMS, &c.

—◆◆—

MARINE INSURANCE POLICY.

No. 1.

THE MARINE
INSURANCE COMPANY.

ESTABLISHED 1836.

No.

£

WHEREAS

represented to us whose Hands are hereunto subscribed and who are Two of the Directors of
THE MARINE INSURANCE COMPANY that
.   interested in or duly authorized as Owner
Agent or otherwise to make the Insurance hereinafter
mentioned and described with THE MARINE INSURANCE
COMPANY and   promised
or otherwise obliged
to pay forthwith for the use of the said Company at the
Office of the said Company the sum of

as a Premium or
Consideration at and after the rate of
per cent., for such Insurance

Now THIS POLICY OF INSURANCE WITNESSETH that in consideration of the premises and of the said Sum of

WE do for ourselves and each of us promise and agree with the said

Executors Administrators and Assigns that the Capital Stock and Funds of the said Company shall according to the provisions of the Deed of Settlement of the said Company be subject and liable to pay and make good and shall be applied to pay and make good all such Losses and Damages hereinafter expressed as may happen to the subject matter of this Policy and may attach to this Policy in respect of the Sum of
Pounds hereby insured which Insurance is hereby declared to be upon

the Ship or Vessel called the
whereof   is at present
Master or whoever shall go for Master of the said Ship or Vessel lost or not lost at and from

AND WE do promise and agree that the Insurance aforesaid shall commence upon the said Ship at and from
                                        and shall continue until
she hath moored at anchor in good safety at
                her Place of Destination and for such period

o

afterwards not exceeding twenty-four hours from such mooring and upon the Freight and Goods or Merchandise on board thereof from the loading of the said Goods or Merchandise on board the said Ship or Vessel at

and until the said Goods or Merchandise be discharged and safely landed at

AND that it shall be lawful for the said Ship or Vessel to proceed and sail to and touch and stay at any Ports or Places whatsoever in the course of her said Voyage for all necessary purposes without prejudice to this Insurance AND touching the Adventures and Perils which the Capital Stock and Funds of the said Company are made liable unto or are intended to be made liable unto by this Insurance they are of the Seas Men-of-War Fire Enemies Pirates Rovers Thieves Jettisons Letters of Mart and Counter Mart Surprisals Takings at Sea Arrests Restraints and Detainments of all Kings Princes and People of what Nation Condition or Quality soever Barratry of the Master and Mariners and of all other Perils Losses and Misfortunes that have or shall come to the Hurt Detriment or Damage of the aforesaid subject matter of this Insurance or any part thereof AND in case of any Loss or Misfortune it shall be lawful to the Insured their Factors Servants and Assigns to sue labour and travel for in and about the Defence Safeguard and Recovery of the aforesaid subject matter of this Insurance or any part thereof without prejudice to this Insurance the charges whereof the Capital Stock and Funds of the said Company shall bear in proportion to the sum hereby insured AND it is declared and agreed that Corn Fish Salt Fruit Flour and Seed shall be and are warranted free from Average unless general or the Ship be stranded and that Sugar Tobacco Hemp Flax Hides and Skins shall be and are warranted free from Average under Five Pounds per Centum that all other Goods also the Ship and Freight shall be and are warranted free from average under Three Pounds per Centum unless general or the Ship be Stranded

PROVIDED NEVERTHELESS that the Capital Stock and Funds of the said Company shall alone be liable according to the provisions of the Deed of Settlement to answer and make good all Claims and Demands whatsoever under or by virtue of this Policy and that no Proprietor of the said Company his or her Heirs Executors or Administrators shall be in anywise subject or liable to any Claims or Demands nor be in anywise charged by reason of this Policy beyond the amount of his or her Share or Shares in the said Capital Stock of the Company it being one of the original or fundamental Principles of the Company that the Responsibility of the Individual Proprietors shall in all Cases be limited to their respective shares in the said Capital Stock.

IN WITNESS whereof WE have hereunto set our hands in London the   day of   186

Examined

Secretary.

INVOICE OF PIASSABA, bought by order and shipped for account and risk of Arthur Robottom, Esq., of Birmingham, per *Florist*, Captain Wainwright, to Liverpool.

R 198 bundles Piassaba, 193 @ 24 per   2,800   542,500

Charges.

Export duty, 193 @ 24 per 3,000 }	581,250	
12% Rs.	69,750	
Ver-o-pezo, 193 @ 20	3,860	
Capatazia, 198 B, 40	7,920	
Rs.	81,530	
Receiving, weighing, and marking.................... }	15,840	
Negro-hire and shipping ...	19,800	
Warehousing and petties ...	11,880	
		129,050
	Rs.	671,550
Commission 5%		33,580
	Rs.	705,130

E. E.

GEB. KALKMANN & Co.

PARA, 18*th February*, 1866.

BILL OF LADING.—SAILING VESSEL.

M B
1 to 6

SHIPPED in good Order, and well conditioned, by MOR-
RISON BROTHERS, of Leghorn, in and upon the good Ship
called the *Foxhound*, whereof is Master for this present
Voyage, *Simms*, and now riding at anchor in the Port of
Leghorn, and bound for *London, Six blocks Marble, C. Ps.*
100, being marked and numbered as in the margin,
and are to be delivered in the like good order and well
conditioned, at the aforesaid Port of *London* (the Act of
God, the Queen's Enemies, Fire, and all and every other
Danger and Accident of the Seas, Rivers, and Navigation, of whatever nature and kind soever, excepted), unto
Order, or to   Assigns, he or they paying Freight
for the said Goods *Twenty Shillings Sterling per ton
of 25 cubic palms, and* 10 %, *Primage.*

IN WITNESS whereof I the said Master or Purser of
the said Ship hath affirmed to three Bills of Lading, all of
this Tenor and Date, the one of which Bills being accomplished, the others to stand void.

Dated in Leghorn the 4th March, 1866.

Measurement (contents) unknown to   R. Simms.

Not accountable for chipped corners and edges.

Endorsed at back :—
                    " Deliver the within,
                        MORRISON BROTHERS."

STEAM-SHIP BILL OF LADING.

SHIPPED, in good order and condition, by MORRISON BROTHERS, in and upon the Steam-ship called the *Volunteer*, whereof is Master for the present Voyage, *Bland*, or whoever else may go as Master in the said Ship, lying in the Port of Leghorn, and bound for London, with liberty to call at any Port or Ports, in any order, *M. B.* 62/78 *Seventeen Blocks Marble, Tons* 11, being marked and numbered as per margin, and to be delivered from the Ship's tackle, where the Ship's responsibility shall cease, in the like good order and condition, at the aforesaid Port of *London*, or so near thereto as she can safely get (the Act of God, the Queen's Enemies, Pirates, Barratry of Master or Mariners, Restraint of Princes and Rulers, Fire at Sea or on Shore, Accidents from Machinery, Boilers, Steam, or any other Accidents of the Seas, Rivers, and Steam Navigation of whatever nature or kind soever, excepted, including all risk of Craft, with liberty to call at any Port or Ports to receive and discharge Cargo, or for any other purpose whatever, and with liberty, in the event of the said Steamer putting back, or into any Port, or otherwise being prevented from any cause from proceeding in the ordinary course of her Voyage, to tranship the Goods by any other Steamer belonging to, or chartered by, the same Owners; with liberty to sail with or without Pilots, and to tow and assist Vessels in all situations).

Unto *Order*, or to his or their Assigns.

Freight and Primage for the said Goods, as per margin, to be paid by the *Consignees at the rate of* 21 *shillings sterling per ton of* 25 *cubic Genoese palms, with* 10 *per cent. Primage,* Lighterage, and Average accustomed.

In Witness whereof, the Master or Agent of the said ship hath affirmed to three Bills of Lading, all of this tenor and date, the one of which Bills being accomplished and delivered up to the Owners or their Agents, in exchange for the Goods, the others to stand void.

Dated in Leghorn, 6th July, 1866.

Weights, Contents, and Value unknown, and not answerable for Leakage, Breakage, or Rust.

The Goods to be discharged from the Ship, as soon as she is ready to unload, into Hulk, or Temporary Depôt, or Lazaretto, or hired Lighter, if necessary, by the Agents of the owners of the Vessel, at the Shippers' or Consignees' risk and expense, after they leave the Ship's tackle, and the Consignees are bound to receive their Goods as they are landed from the Crafts or Lighters, the Agents of the Steamer having power to land the Goods on the Quays, Calate, or Gates of Portofranco; the Steamer or Agents being in no way answerable for damage to Goods from Wet, Rain or any other cause, whilst on board of or after discharge from Lighters.

All fines and expenses, or losses by detention of Vessel or Cargo, caused by incorrect marking of the Packages, or by incomplete or incorrect description or weight (or of any other particulars required by the authorities at the Port of Discharge), upon either the Packages or the Bill of Lading, shall be paid by the Shippers or Consignees of the Goods, and the Shipowner has a lien upon the Goods until the payment of all such costs and charges.

All Quarantine Expenses upon the Goods, of whatever nature and kind, to be likewise paid by the Shippers or Consignees of the Goods.

The Owners of this Ship will not be accountable for Gold, Silver, Bullion, Specie, Jewellery, or Precious Stones, unless Bills of Lading are signed for such Goods and the value declared in the Bills of Lading.

In case of the Blockade or Interdict of the Port of Discharge, or if, without such Blockade or Interdict, the entering of the Port of Discharge should be considered unsafe, by reason of war or disturbances, the Master to have the option of landing the Goods at any other Port which he may consider safe, at Shipper's risk and expense ; and on the goods being placed in charge of any Mercantile Agent, or of the British Consul, and a letter being put into the Post-Office addressed to the Shippers or Consignees, if named, stating the landing and with whom deposited, the Goods to be at the Shipper's risk and expense, and the Master and Owners discharged from all responsibility.　In the event of Quarantine, the goods to be discharged on arrival into Quarantine Depôt, Hulk, Lighter, or other Vessels necessary for the Ship's dispatch at the Consignees' risk and expense ; or, should this be impracticable, or the Vessel not admitted, the Master to have the option, and is hereby authorized, to land the

Cargo at the nearest safe Port to which the Vessel is bound, at the risk and expense of the Consignees.

All charges for Stamps to be borne by the Consignees.

For the CAPTAIN,

MORRISON BROTHERS, Agents.

Freight on Tons 11, @ 21s. per ton.........	£11	11	0
Ten per cent. primage	1	3	1
Total payable in London	£12	14	1

A PROMISSORY NOTE.

LONDON, *Aug.* 14, 1866.

£150.

Three Months after date I promise to pay to Mr. Jas. Jackson, or his order, One hundred and fifty pounds, for value received.

EDWARD PHILLIPS,
504, Regent Street.

[This should be drawn on a 2s. bill stamp.]

Marks.	Numbers.	Boxes.	Casks.	Tons.	Cwt.	Qrs.	Lbs.
B S	12 Reg. Stoves...				11	3	15
D & S	12 Ranges in 29 } Pieces ...... }				18	1	4

FOREIGN BILL OF EXCHANGE.

MALTA, *the 3rd March*, 1866.   For £75.

ON DEMAND of this sole of Exchange (others date unpaid), Pay to the Order of Messrs. James Bell and Company, the sum of Seventy-five Pounds sterling, value received, which place with or without further advice to the account of

Accepted, payable at the Exchange Bank, 79, Lombard Street. P. L. SIMMONDS.

WALTER STRICKLAND.

To P. L. SIMMONDS, Esq.,
      8, Winchester   Street,
                    London, S.W.

Endorsed—Pay Messrs. John Ranking & Co.—James Bell & Co.

COASTING BILL OF LADING.

SHIPPED, in good order and condition, by PHILLIPS & SON, in and upon the good Ship or Vessel called the *Clyde*, whereof is Master for this present Voyage *Peter McKay*, and now riding at anchor in the *Harbour of Grangemouth,* and bound for *London,* to say, *One Ton Ten Hundredweight and Nineteen Pounds of Castings,* being marked and numbered as in the margin,* and are to be delivered in the like good order and well-conditioned at the aforesaid Port of *London* (the Act of God, the Queen's Enemies, Fire, and all and every other Dangers and Accidents of the Seas, Rivers, and Navigation, of whatever Nature and Kind soever, excepted), unto Mr. WILLIAM HADEN, 2, Brabant Court, London, or to *his* Assigns, *Shippers* paying Freight for the said goods with Primage and Average accustomed.

IN WITNESS whereof, the Master or Purser of the said Ship or Vessel hath affirmed to *three* Bills of Lading, all of this Tenor and Date, the one of which Bills being accomplished, the other two to stand void.

Dated in Grangemouth,
　　　　7th August, 1866.

Breakage excepted.

Pro A. GAULT,

JAS. GRAHAM.

* See opposite page.

SHIPPING BILL

For British Manufactures, Foreign Goods free of Duty, or on which all Duties have been Paid, and are not to be Drawnback.

Ship's Name.	Whether British or Foreign Ship; if Foreign, the Country.	Master's Name.	Port or Place of Destination

Marks and Nos.	No. of Pack ages.	Description of Packages.	Quantity, Quality, and Description of Goods.	The value of British Goods & of Foreign Goods, formerly charged with Duty at Value (if any.)		
				£.	s.	d.
Total Packages.			Total Value £			

I declare the quantity and description of the British Goods above mentioned to be correctly stated and the Value of the same to be

(Signed)_____Exporter or Agent.

Station of Clearance,

(Countersigned) _____Searcher.

Dated this   day of   18

INVOICE OF SUNDRY GOODS, shipped per *Hero of Alma*, from London, for Kingston, Jamaica.

Mark.

B L S

1/4	4 Hhds. Ironmongery, as per bill	100	15	7
5/11	7 Chests Glass Ware ...	71	10	0
12/13	2 Bundles Iron Ware ...	50	10	0
14	1 Case of Hats and Bonnets	21	8	6
15/16	2 Casks Saddlery	18	9	1
17/22	3 Puncheons of Hams and 3 of Tongues ...	112	16	7

                                               —375 9 9

Charges.

Cartage & Dock dues	1	3	5
Sundry Shipping charges	2	16	10

                                          —— 4 0 3

Commission, $2\frac{1}{2}$ °/$_0$.................................... 9 9 8

Insurance at £4. 10s. & 3 °/$_0$...	12	6	0
Stamp Duty	0	12	6
Commission, $\frac{1}{2}$ °/$_0$..................	2	1	0

                                        —— 14 19 6

                                     £403 19 2

E. E.

CHARTER PARTY.

LIVERPOOL, *Aug.* 16, 1866.

IT IS THIS DAY MUTUALLY AGREED, between ALFRED DUNBAR & SONS, *Masters and Owners* of the good Ship or Vessel called the *Star of Africa, schooner,* of the measurement of 250 Tons Register, or thereabouts, and JAMES MORTON & SONS, *Agents for the Guinea Company, Limited,* Merchants, that the said Ship being tight, staunch and strong, and in every way fitted for the Voyage, shall, with all convenient speed, sail and proceed to *the ports of Accra and Lagos, on the West Coast of Africa,* or as near thereunto as she may safely get, and there load from the factors of the said Merchants a full and complete cargo of *Palm Oil, Kernels, Cotton, or other lawful Produce, which is to be brought to and taken from alongside at Merchant's risk and expense,* and not exceeding what she can reasonably stow and carry, over and above her tackle, apparel, provisions, and furniture, and being so loaded shall therewith proceed to *the Port of Liverpool,* or as near thereunto as she may safely get, and deliver the same on being paid freight, *to the Agents of the Guinea Company, Limited. Restraint of Princes and Rulers, the Act of God, the Queen's Enemies, Fire, and all and every other dangers and accidents of the Seas, Rivers, and Navigation of whatever nature and kind soever during the said voyage always excepted.*

Freight to be paid on the right delivery of the cargo, half *on return of vessel to Liverpool, and the remaining* half *by bills at six months.* *Thirty-six running* days (*Sundays excepted*) to be allowed the said Merchant (if the Ship be not sooner despatched) for *loading.* *Notice in writing to be given the Factors or Agents of the Company by the Captain of the Ship, when he is ready to commence loading,* and *not exceeding ten* days on Demurrage over and above the said laying days at £5 *sterling* per day. *Time occupied in changing ports not to count.* Penalty for non-performance of this agreement, estimated amount of freight.

Witness to the signature of

Edwd. Wright.

James Morton & Sons,
Agents for the
Guinea Co. Limited.

Witness to the signature of

Henry Roberts.

Alfred Dunbar & Sons.

INLAND BILL OF EXCHANGE.

LONDON, *Aug.* 16, 1836.

£214. 10*s.* 6*d.*

Two Months after date pay to my order the sum of Two hundred and fourteen pounds ten shillings and sixpence, for value received.

E. SMITH.

To Messrs. ALBEMARLE & Co.,
  Regent Street.

If drawn on a proper bill-stamp, and written across the face, thus—

Accepted, ALBEMARLE & Co.,
Payable at Bank of England Branch,
Burlington Street,

it is a valid document, and becomes negociable.

NOVELS AT ONE SHILLING.

(Postage 3d.)

BY CAPTAIN MARRYAT.

Peter Simple.
The King's Own.
Midshipman Easy.
Rattlin the Reefer.
The Pacha of Many Tales.

Newton Forster.
Jacob Faithful.
Japhet in Search of a Father.
The Dog-Fiend.
The Poacher.

The Phantom Ship.
Percival Keene.
Valerie.
Frank Mildmay.
Olla Podrida.
Monsieur Violet.

BY J. FENIMORE COOPER.

The Last of the Mohicans.
The Spy.
Lionel Lincoln.
The Deerslayer.
The Pathfinder.
The Bravo.

The Waterwitch.
The Two Admirals.
The Red Rover.
Satanstoe.
Afloat and Ashore.
Wyandotte.
The Headsman.

Homeward Bound.
The Sea Lions.
Precaution.
Mark's Reef.
Ned Myers.
The Heidenmauer.

BY G. P. R. JAMES.

Agincourt.
Attila.
Margaret Graham.
Delaware.

Henry of Guise.
Dark Scenes.
The Smuggler.
Rose D'Albret.

John Marston Hall.
Beauchamp.
Arrah Neil.
My Aunt Pontypool.

BY ALEXANDRE DUMAS.

The Three Musketeers.
Twenty Years After.
Doctor Basilius.
The Twin Captains.
Captain Paul.
Memoirs of a Physician. 2 vols.
The Queen's Necklace.
The Chevalier de Maison Rouge.
The Countess de Charny.

Monte Cristo. 2 vols.
Nanon; or, Woman's War.
The Two Dianas.
The Black Tulip.
The Forty-Five Guardsmen.
Taking the Bastille. 2 vols.
Chicot the Jester.
The Conspirators.
Ascanio.

BY W. H. AINSWORTH.

Windsor Castle.
Tower of London.
The Miser's Daughter.
Rookwood.
Old St. Paul's.
Crichton.

Guy Fawkes.
The Spendthrift.
James the Second.
The Star Chamber.
The Flitch of Bacon.
Mervyn Clitheroe.

Lancashire Witches.
Ovingdean Grange.
St. James's.
Auriol.
Jack Sheppard.

Published by George Routledge and Sons.

4

Novels at One Shilling.—*Continued.*
By Various Authors.

Violet the Danseuse.
The Royal Favourite. *Mrs. Gore.*
Joe Wilson's Ghost. *Banim.*
Ambassador's Wife. *Mrs. Gore.*
The Old Commodore.
Author of "Rattlin the Reefer."
Cinq Mars. *De Vigny.*
Ladder of Life. *A. B. Edwards.*
My Brother's Keeper.
Miss Wetherell.
The Scarlet Letter. *Hawthorne.*
Respectable Sinners.
The House of the Seven Gables.
Hawthorne.
Whom to Marry. *Mayhew.*
Henpecked Husband. *Lady Scott.*
The Family Feud. *Thos. Cooper.*
Nothing but Money.
T. S. Arthur.
Letter-Bag of the Great Western.
Sam Slick.
Moods. *Louisa M. Alcott.*
Singleton Fontenoy. *J. Hannay.*
Kindness in Women.
Mohegan Maiden, and other Tales
Stories of Waterloo.

Zingra the Gipsy.
My Brother's Wife.
Tom Jones.
The Duke.
My Cousin Nicholas. [sion.
Northanger Abbey, and Persua-
Land and Sea Tales.
The Warlock.
Echoes from the Backwoods.
Balthazar. *Balzac.*
Eugenie Grandet.
The Vicar of Wakefield.
The Sparrowgrass Papers.
A Seaside Sensation. *C. Ross.*
A Week with Mossoo. *Chas. Ross.*
Miss Tomkins' Intended.
Arthur Sketchley.
On the Road. *B. Hemyng.*
A Bundle of Crowquills.
The Hidden Path.
A Sailor's Adventures.
The Medical Student. *A. Smith.*
Love Tales. *G. H. Kingsley.*
The Backwoods Bride.
Kent the Ranger.
Ennui. *Edgeworth.*

BEADLE'S LIBRARY.
Price 6d. each. (*Postage* 1d.)

Alice Wilde.
The Frontier Angel.
Malaeska.
Uncle Ezekiel.
Massasoit's Daughter.
Bill Biddon, Trapper.
Backwoods Bride.
Sybil Chase.
Monowano, the Shaw-
nee Spy.
Brethren of the Coast.
King Barnaby.
The Forest Spy.
The Far West.
Riflemen of Miami.
Alicia Newcombe.
The Hunter's Cabin.

The Block House.
Esther; or, The Ore-
gon Trail.
The Gold Hunters.
Mabel Meredith.
The Scout.
The King's Man.
Kent the Ranger.
The Peon Prince.
Laughing Eyes.
Mahaska, the Indian
Queen.
The Slave Sculptor.
Myrtle.
Indian Jem.
The Wrecker's Bride.
The Cave Child.

The Lost Trail.
Joe Davis's Client.
The Cuban Heiress.
The Hunter's Escape.
The Silver Bugle.
Pomfret's Ward.
Quindaro.
The Rival Scouts.
On the Plains.
Star Eyes.
The Mad Skipper.
Little Moccasin.
The Doomed Hunter.
Eph. Peters.
The Fugitives.
Big-Foot the Guide.

Published by George Routledge and Sons.